Abby Hemenway's

VERMONT

Abby Hemenway's
VERMONT

Unique Portrait of a State

by

ABBY MARIA HEMENWAY

Selected and Edited by

Brenda C. Morrissey

THE STEPHEN GREENE PRESS
BRATTLEBORO, VERMONT

This book has been produced in the United States of America:
designed by R. L. Dothard Associates, composed by
The Heffernan Press, printed and bound by
Halliday Lithograph Corporation. It is published by
The Stephen Greene Press, Brattleboro, Vermont 05301.

Library of Congress Catalog Card Number: 75-173401
International Standard Book Number: 0-8289-0144-9

Acknowledgments

The publisher is indebted to Esther Munroe Swift—historian, editor, and author—for the Chronology at the end of this book, and to Walter R. Hard, Jr., Editor of *Vermont Life* Magazine, for permission to include as an introduction Janet Greene's "To Meet Miss Abby Hemenway," which first appeared in the Winter 1960 issue of *Vermont Life* under the title "The Woman Who Told Everything."

Contents

Editor's Foreword

ABBY HEMENWAY's *Vermont Gazetteer* has long been a favorite of genealogists studying their family trees, and of town historians seeking information about their communities.

Although most Vermonters have not read Abby's *Gazetteer*—perhaps discouraged by its small print and interminable sermons and tributes—many have heard of the books and remember a story or two from them.

This anthology might thus be called "Abby Without Eyestrain."

My approach to editing has not been scholarly. Instead, I have chosen articles that seemed to convey the tenor of life during the first 140 years of Vermont's history—from the earliest settlement through the Civil War, which is the span covered by the *Gazetteer*.

Here will be found accounts of the hardships endured by early settlers, encounters with Indians, political campaigns, schooling, church-state relationships, land speculation, samples of poetry, and independent opinions.

If one theme runs through Abby, it is that Vermonters—ranging from lawyers and teachers, to politicians and tourists—had an opinion on almost any subject. A strain of Vermont chauvinism may also be found. Many of her correspondents wondered why young Vermonters could possibly wish to seek their fortunes elsewhere. The answer, of course, lay in the lack of economic opportunity to be found in Vermont, together with the harsh climate and the rocky terrain.

This book is divided into five roughly chronological sections: early settlement up to 1775; the Revolutionary era; the Federal period—1791 to about 1825; the "age of ferment" from the mid-1820's to 1860; and the Civil War decade.

In trying to select only the best of the *Gazetteer*, I found the quality of contributions to it quite uneven. One consequence is that several of the selections are not in strict chronological order. Development, too, had proceeded at an uneven pace across the state—settlement in remote areas of Northern Vermont, for example, did not take place until the last quarter of the eighteenth century—and several of the best accounts of pioneer life are set in this later era. Thus, Seth Hubbell's fascinating narrative of his difficult life in Wolcott in 1789 is included in the chapter on early settlement, rather than in the section on the Revolutionary era. The hardships he endured were very likely similar to those experienced by settlers in other regions a half century before.

Ethan Allen and his exploits with the Green Mountain Boys are widely known, so I decided not to include detailed accounts of their adventures in this book. It seemed more important to focus on lesser-known events and personalities of Vermont's early history. For this reason, I selected a first-person narrative by a citizen-soldier at the Battle of Plattsburgh in 1814, an event in a war that had a great impact upon life in Vermont, particularly along the Canadian border.

Abby is also interesting for what she chose to de-emphasize. Although Vermont elected a governor on the Anti-Masonic ticket in 1831, the controversy is soft-pedaled. Brigham Young and Joseph Smith (both born in Vermont) earn only brief mention, and Mormonism itself is treated in a markedly casual way.

Perhaps a Victorian sense of propriety dictated the omission of some subjects which she may have felt would cause embarrassment to people still living when the volumes of the *Gazetteer* were published, and who might have regretted their earlier flirtation with particular movements.

To those who complain that their favorite stories are omitted here, I can only say there is material enough in the *Gazetteer* for another selection of excerpts. Let them read the five volumes and choose their own portrait of Vermont as it was!

In editing this book I would like to acknowledge the assistance of the Vermont Historical Society staff, particularly Linda Houghton, Paula Sambel and the Director, Charles T. Morrissey, who in the rôle of husband encouraged me to keep plugging away; to Donna Sambel, who on short notice agreed to type it; to Janet Greene, who must have wondered whether the manuscript would ever be forthcoming; and to Michael Collins Morrissey and Susan Katharine Morrissey, who now will be able to persuade their mother to go skiing without her worrying about Abby being neglected at home.

B.C.M.

Originating locale and volume number references to the original *Gazeteer* for the excerpts presented here are indicated by the marginal glosses.

To Meet
Miss Abby Hemenway

NEAR THE BASE of her family's stone in Ludlow Cemetery is the legend ABBY MARIA HEMENWAY, OCT. 7, 1828, FEB. 24, 1890, and the wording, though too short on details to please her as history, would have suited her on another score: it gives a beginning and it gives an ending. And if there was one thing Miss Hemenway wanted in her lonely, fanatical life, it was to tell a story from beginning to end.

She almost did. Goaded by her ideal of preserving a past "too rich and, in many points, or some, too unique or romantic to lose," she labored for thirty years to record the story of Vermont county by county and town by town, and died with one county still to go. The result is a sociologists' dream. *The Vermont Historical Gazetteer*, compiled and edited by Abby Maria Hemenway, embraces five volumes containing six thousand pages and four million words and every fact she could get her hands on.

With its first installment her project was hailed as an "historic monument to the Green Mountain State such as no other State has"; this judgment is still valid a century later—and so is the view that it was like "history shoveled in." Work of genius or a mishmash, the *Gazetteer* is considered Item No. 1 among today's collectors of Vermontiana.

Abby Hemenway traveled in any weather to collect her material. She researched. She enlisted contributing authors—three, six, ten to a town; she flattered or wheedled; when reasons failed, she used extortion, and never turned a hair. Lack of money, not of energy, made the *Gazetteer*'s progress eccentric: she had to sell enough of one volume to pay printers working on the next one. So she sized up her market and devised her come-ons, committed burglary, even fled her Green Mountains to escape from debts. "I understand that you had trouble with Miss Hemenway," a Chicago lawyer wrote home to her creditors shortly after she died. "Everybody did."

There is little direct information about what she was like, but certainly Abby was no trouble in her early years.

Records show that she was the fourth of ten children born to Daniel and Abigail Barton Hemenway of Ludlow, and family stories mention her as a bright little thing, honing her wits on discussions of such grave problems as Abolition, and trained to marshal her ideas and present them, unflinching, in prose or verse. It is said that she taught in a district school at the age of fourteen, well before she enrolled in Ludlow's Black River Academy in 1846. She studied hard and worked hard for the next five or six years, was a leader in the Baptist Church, and found time to star in dramatic productions, plummy with uplift and sensibility, put on by the local Ladies' Association for Mental and Other Improvement.

Details of her life are even more shadowy from around 1852 to 1858. She spent three not very happy years as a teacher in Michigan, where she wrote verses of a particularly emotional sort. She returned to Ludlow inspired to exhibit the condition of "general poetic literature" in her home state, and published *Poets and Poetry of Vermont* in 1858. The anthology enjoyed two highly successful printings because this bookish old maid—Abby was thirty by now—had an instinct for merchandising that was a hundred years ahead of its time.

She solicited poems through notices put in county newspapers, thereby receiving three thousand manuscript pages and some fine advance publicity. Cannily she named an "examining committee" to approve her one hundred and ten selections, which mirrored the current taste for doggerel and sentimental ballads, with an occasional flash of competent verse. Interest in her book was heightened, too, by a caustic dissent regarding its merits. Yet *Poets* would have had a market without fanfare or controversy, for Abby Maria was passionately sincere. Poetry was noble, it was beautiful; Vermont was wonderful. Her public agreed—and what more genteel occupation for a female than to preserve the poesy of such a region?

Her next project was not welcomed as being so decorous.

"We had 'Poets and Poetry of Vermont' well off [our] hands," she wrote later, "and were looking around for something of a Vermont character to do."

What she found to do was to compile a history of her state different from any before or since. There existed several excellent chronicles of Vermont. Among them, Zadock Thompson's *History of the State of Vermont From Its Earliest Settlement to the Close of the Year 1832* (Burlington, 1833) still is, in two of its three parts, unsurpassed as a standard reference. However, Abby felt that his third section, the two hundred-odd pages called a gazetteer, should be amplified.

Local and personal: this was the answer. Let Thompson give Vermont's early civil and natural history, but let her set down the human details of each town's past before it was too late, before the material became "daily more indistinct and irrecoverable." She would get trustworthy leaders in every community to collaborate and she would publish their accounts as pamphlets issued quarterly, by counties and alphabetically, for twenty-five cents. She would start with Addison. Her home county of Windsor might be an easier beginning but by rights it should come at the end, and anyway Addison had the only full-fledged historical society in the state and besides it had Middlebury College. Fourteen counties meant three and one-half years. She must start right away.

Flushed with praise for launching *Poets and Poetry*, she ordered a thousand circulars inviting contributors to her wonderful design —and was told that her plan was "not suitable for a woman."

Disapproval came from no less august a body than the faculty of Middlebury College. The county historical society was then sixteen years old and had forty members. If forty males had not yet produced such a history, how could Miss Hemenway possibly...? She would break down before she was half through the county. And maybe her idea carried an overtone of women's equality. At any rate the professors had an alternative: a nice anthology of prose, for which they happened to have some ideas.

But history was what she was after, and the histories of Addison's twenty-three towns Miss Hemenway eventually got. She turned the flank of masculine superiority, parried the blows of indifference or delay, and on July 4, 1860, published the *Vermont Quarterly Gazetteer*, No. 1, "embracing the civil, ecclesiastical, biographical and military history of each town" in Addison County. In her exhilaration over getting it done she minimized her troubles in gingering authors or selling subscriptions. By midsummer of 1860 she was already in debt, she was behind her schedule, and she was more certain than ever that the *Gazetteer* should be finished, regardless. The pattern for the rest of her life was established.

The Civil War naturally slowed her down, and five more issues, still titled as quarterlies and still not making expenses, appeared over the next three years and dealt with Bennington, Caledonia and Chittenden counties. After the issue of August 1863 she suspended the *Gazetteer* until the war would be over.

Meanwhile Abby collected another book of poetry, published in 1863 as *Songs of the War*. It contained seventy-three entries, many of which she had clipped from newspapers, and had poems by Oliver Wendell Holmes, Thomas Bailey Aldrich, William Cullen Bryant and Henry Wadsworth Longfellow.

The following year Miss Hemenway announced that she had been converted to the Roman Catholic faith. It is impossible to trace the steps by which this daughter of a rather sternly evangelical Baptist family arrived at her decision; it is equally hard to assess the strain her conversion was to place on her dealings with many Protestant clergymen whom she needed as authors for the *Gazetteer*. The history tabled until war's end, she moved to Burlington to make her home with Mrs. Lydia Clarke Meech, an elderly widow who was also a recent convert to Catholicism, and to write the first of three books of religious verse.

Then in 1867 appeared the next work on her history, this time as Volume I of *The Vermont Historical Gazetteer*. It covered Essex County in addition to the material already presented in the quarterlies. With this section bound in permanent form it was now possible to prevaluate the finished work—and to discover, in its 1,096 unself-conscious pages, what Miss A. M. Hemenway, Publisher, was really like.

In her preface she had said, "Vermonters are New Englanders, and like naturally to know about a thing that interests them, from beginning to end." From this major premise she reasoned that, since the personality of Vermont so interested her, everyone else in the state shared her thirst for details. Her hope was to tell everything: she pursued it with the unleavened single-mindedness that hallmarked the emancipated Yankee spinster of the middle eighteen-hundreds.

Apparently she gave free rein to her nearly four hundred contributors to Volume I, for she jumbled masterly political resumés and countermarches with church foundings and geology, repulses of Indians and bears, and lists of especially long-lived residents. First settlers, first charters, military rosters; merchant tonnage on Lake Champlain and local eccentrics and sermons and hardships among the heathen—she told it all. When a town's correspondents failed to produce, the Editor obliged by quoting Thompson and adding tidbits clipped from the papers. Sometimes the result was a mere rundown of important events; or, as in the case of Vergennes, she achieved altitude with an invocation to Labor, Worship and Nature before imparting the statistic that the falls of the Otter River have a descent of thirty-seven feet.

The pages are spangled with asterisks leading down to her footnotes, and in these asides she is even more self-revealing. Painfully conscientious, she gave credit for every source. It is hard to believe that she cut or reorganized the scripts, but "Oaths are omitted," she might note primly, or wonder which of two infants was really the first one born in a certain town. She cross-referred; she gave pats for good conduct, and praised support of the *Gazetteer* (although thirteen pages of back-matter also carried names of patrons and favorable reviews by the press).

Thus through her editorial approach, never altered for the rest of the history, Abby Hemenway emerges as a brilliant woman, naïve despite her shrewdness, indefatigable and dedicated.

Life in Burlington seemed to ensure an orderly progress toward her goal. Abby had a beau, a Methodist minister who admired her to the point of waiving differences of religious opinion if she would consent to marry him; when he became too importunate she suggested lightly that her sister Carrie take him off her hands. There is no indication that she preened, even a little, over her conquest, though she did like his interest in the *Gazetteer*. In 1871 she was able to produce the histories of Franklin, Grand Isle, Lamoille and Orange counties as Volume II.

Then Mrs. Meech died, leaving her a life interest in her house. This generosity was to embroil Miss Hemenway in a long and bitter lawsuit with the stepson of her benefactress; he contested the will, charging undue influence. Publication of Volume III, Orleans and Rutland counties, was delayed until 1877. She won the litigation a year or so later, but with her Pyrrhic victory—she spent a large part of the eventual inheritance defending herself—her affairs began to disintegrate.

Sometime before, she had had to sell her title to the second and third volumes and thereby forgo the income she needed so badly. The only way to finance her coming Volume IV on Washington County was to ask the state legislature to underwrite it. This the General Assemblies of '78 and '80 agreed to do, but in a manner so modest and so restricted that Abby was to receive less than $500 from the State of Vermont for the *Gazetteer*. Nevertheless she managed to get out the fourth volume in 1882, dedicating it to the legislature with what even she must have felt was a desperate hope, mortgaging it in advance and cutting corners everywhere except in the integrity of its contents. In the next few months she must have labored without rest to drum up advance sales and prepare the two more volumes that would complete her project. Always plain, her face became permanently stamped with a combination of force and anxiety.

In March 1883 all of Volume IV, bound and unbound, was seized by her creditors and stored for safekeeping in a Montpelier bindery until she should pay some of her bills. This was too much. They must have known that without her copies to sell she could never pay; or worse- -that with no more money she might not continue the history. Why could people *never* see?

She went to the bindery in the night and took, by main force, the copies of Volume IV.

Her finaglings had been one thing, out-and-out burglary was another. Yet Abby Maria Hemenway was changed, whether or not her mind was really unbalanced. She was finally convinced that she, by herself, must be responsible for the *Gazetteer*. She would keep collecting material and she would never stop wooing subscribers. She would set the text in type piecemeal, with her own hands if she had to, and sell it pamphlet by pamphlet to individual towns until she could bind Windham and Windsor counties as the fifth and sixth volumes, and her life's work would be finished.

This was her program when she sought refuge back home in Ludlow, and she followed it after she moved to Chicago beyond reach of her creditors. There she lived as a recluse, doggedly building the *Gazetteer*. A fire destroyed the printshop where she had part of the manuscript and some town histories already in pages. She reported the tragedy halfway through the body of Volume V:

"May 25, 1886, parts of Windham county Vol. V., including 16 pages of Brookline with the type, stock, paper, etc. were utterly consumed [by fire], and no insurance; to refurnish... we have worked at a disadvantage, but believe us, Vermont, hard for you this time, so in the midst of otherwise deserved criticism remember mercy."

Her style had become eccentric—perhaps from hysteria, and who could blame her?—but it holds no trace of self-pity. There was simply no time for it. She replaced the burned sections of Windham County, setting in type each day the scripts she had edited the night before, and started arranging contributions for the book on Windsor, the final region her history need cover.

Volume V of the *Gazetteer* was three-fourths done when she died alone in her room on the 24th of February, 1890. Her sister Carrie completed the text from material on hand and published it for Abby the following year. Three decades after her death the State of Vermont awoke to the value of Miss Hemenway's treasure and authorized an Index to the *Gazetteer* at a cost of $12,000.

But nothing could be done about Windsor, and no one has set down the rest of the story that she wanted, with all her heart, to tell.

JANET GREENE

The author acknowledges help from many sources, chief among them Volumes I through V of The Vermont Historical Gazetteer; *and* Abby Maria Hemenway (1827–1890) Historian, Anthologist and Poet *by Frances Harriet Babb (Sister Mary Michaelis of the Confraternity of Christian Doctrine Center in Jamestown, North Dakota), Division of Graduate Study, University of Maine, 1939; and information supplied by Rensse Kolvoord of The Old Settler Book Shop in Walpole, New Hampshire.*

Abby Hemenway's

VERMONT

1

Early Settlement to 1775

Samuel de Champlain the first European to set foot in Vermont—at Isle La Motte in 1609 : First permanent English settlement in the state—at Fort Dummer in 1724, when Massachusetts decided to protect its western frontier : Land in Vermont was granted too many times, by kings, governors, and land speculators : In 1764, after the French and Indian War, the question of whether New York or New Hampshire "owned" Vermont was paramount : Early settlers faced hardships ranging from climate to disease to an invasion of caterpillars.

AMID COUNTLESS HARDSHIPS and privations the first settlers laid the foundations of this community. It was not all done as we could have wished—not all with the wisest forecast of the future. But they did, nevertheless, a great and stern work; into that work we have entered. They sowed, often in sadness; we reap in joy. Their work is done; ours is yet on our hands. These hills and these valleys, the fertile soil of which they laid open to the sun with the river that winds among them and the grand settings of the mountains, were beautiful to them. They are beautiful, exceedingly beautiful to us. Verily the lines are fallen to us in pleasant places. We have a goodly heritage.

*Waterbury
Washington Co.
Vol. IV*

The first settler of Waterbury was James Marsh, a native of
Canaan, Ct. He had been a soldier in the French war. In the early
part of the Revolutionary war he sold his place in Canaan and
moved to Cornwall, Ct. Soon after this he was drafted as a soldier
in the Revolution. Having a large family of small children, and
his wife being very feeble, he hired a young man as a substitute,
paying him $100. To pay this sum, and with the hope of escaping
service as a minute man, to which he had been enrolled, he sold
his place in Cornwall and bought a right of land in Bath, N. H.,
and one in Waterbury.

The right in Waterbury was purchased of a Mr. Steele, of New
Milford, and deeded in 1780. Soon after this he moved to Bath
and commenced a settlement, in the meantime having buried his
wife and married again. After living there some 2 years, he found
the title to his land in Bath was bad, and he resolved to begin a
settlement in Waterbury, having the assurance that several others
would begin settlements about the same time. In the Spring of
1783 he came on, selected his right, which covered much of the
site of the present village—cleared a small piece of land, and having planted it with corn, returned.

In the fall he came and harvested his crop, putting it into a
rude crib for next year's use. The next spring he came with his
family to the old fort in Corinth, where he left his wife and five
of his eight children, and came on to Waterbury with the remaining three, viz.: Elias, James and Irene, making the journey on
snowshoes, and drawing his provisions and effects on a hand-sled.
He took possession of the surveyors' cabin.

To his dismay he found the corn, so carefully stored the fall
before, was nearly all gone. Bears, Indians or travelers, had taken
well nigh the whole. Relying upon his supply of corn, he had
taken little provision with him and there was none in the shape
of grain, short of a return to Corinth. Hunting and fishing were

his only resource. The last of May, having made an additional clearing, and nearly finished planting his corn, he left his children and returned to Corinth for the remainder of his family, expecting to be absent one week, and leaving provision barely for that time.

During this first summer, this family lived many weeks on wild onions, cooked in the milk of their one cow, the father often gone for many days, in the fruitless endeavor to procure provision. The only occasional relief they had until their corn was harvested, was in the killing of a moose or bear, which in summer could rarely be done. That summer Mr. Marsh built his log-house on his clearing, a little to the west of the graveyard hill, and moved into it. His crop of corn raised near the river was fine, but after he had secured some 20 bushels of it, a flood came and destroyed the remainder. So that for nearly 2 years they lived much of the time on the flesh of the moose, deer and bear. Much of the little grain they had, which was procured in the settlements in Richmond, Williston and Jericho, and brought home on the back, was paid for with the skins of these animals and those of the beaver.

MARK & DAVID NORRIS.

In the Spring of 1793, these cousins supplied themselves with provisions sufficient, as they supposed, to last them through their Spring's work, when they were expecting to return to Peacham for a while. They had no such thing as a team or even a hoe to work with; but with their axes they hewed out wooden hoe-blades from maple chips, hardened them in the fire, and took saplings for handles. With these they hoed in, on Nathaniel's ground, two acres of wheat; but Saturday night came, when they had sowed only *one* acre, and they found they had only provisions enough to last them one day longer. What should they do? Neither of them were professors of religion, but they had been trained to keep the Sabbath day. However, they now held a

Hardwick
Caledonia Co.
Vol. 1

council, concluded that it was a "work of necessity," and hoed in the second and last acre on the Sabbath. "We shall see," said Mark and David, "whether this acre will not yield as well as the other." But Nathaniel was troubled in conscience. Reaping time came; the proceeds of the two acres were stacked separately, and the time for comparing drew near. But the comparison was never made. The stack which came of the Sabbath day's work took fire from a clearing near by, and every straw and kernel was burned.

DAVID HAINES

Cabot
Washington Co.
Vol. IV

commenced on the farm south of George Gould's, so long occupied by his son Wm. Haines, in 1797. When he came to town he was not possessed of a great amount of cash, it may be inferred by the fact he was the owner of two pair of pants and two shirts, and he swapped one shirt and one pair of pants for a hoe and axe to begin work with.

Burke
Caledonia Co.
Vol. 1

Sometimes these cabins would have no chimney save a few boards fastened together in a conical form through which to convey the smoke. Sometimes they would have backs, as they were called, built against the logs at one end of their dwellings; but many were destitute of this appendage, and had nothing for a substitute but logs of wood, which when burnt away were replaced by others. Oftentimes these wooden chimneys would take fire; but, to use the common adage, "Necessity is the mother of invention." Most families had an instrument familiarly called a *"squirt-gun,"* of a large size, through which a considerable quantity of water could be emitted to any part of their dwellings. This was the only *engine* made use of in those days for extinguishing fire in their dwellings, and reminds the writer of an anecdote which he heard related many years ago.

At a certain time, Lemuel Walter, the first inhabitant of the town, was sitting at his table in his log cabin, with a wooden chimney, at noonday, taking his frugal meal, when a stranger on horseback rode up to his door, and with an earnest voice enquired, "Sir, do you know that your house is on fire?" Ah, said the owner, well, no matter, I will see to it as soon as I have finished my dinner. "But," said the stranger, "your house will all be in flames before that time." Be not alarmed, sir, said Walter, I am used to fire and have no fears. Thank you, sir for your trouble. "If you are disposed to stay there and let your house burn down over your head," rejoined the stranger, "it is no business of mine," and rode off, and left the owner to take care of his own house. Whereupon, Walter deliberately took his *squirt-gun* and soon extinguished the fire.

Burke The most hardy of the veteran settlers would resort thither on
Caledonia Co. snow-shoes as soon as a sufficient depth of snow had fallen, and
Vol. 1 surprise and slay [moose], and after dressing them select the best
part of the flesh for food, and carry it on their backs a distance of
7 or 8 miles, through the wilderness, to their homes. Not un-
frequently a man would carry a burden of 100 pounds. But they
soon grew wise by experience, and furnished themselves with a
kind of *hand sled* made expressly for the purpose, the timber of
which was made very light, and the runners, being 5 or 6 inches
in width, prevented their sinking in the snow to a very great
depth. On these a man would draw more than double the quantity
that he could carry on his back, and the labor was not so hard.
These kinds of sleds are used by many at the present time in this
vicinity, and still retain the name of *moose-sleds*.

Lincoln For many years there resided in this town one of those eccentric
Addison Co. beings, compounded of shiftlessness and oddity, spiced with a
Vol. 1 knack at extempore rhyming. One time McComber, our present
hero, was lounging around a new tavern, recently fitted up from
an old building where meetings had been formerly held. The
landlord preferring his departure before dinner, plainly hinted
his room would be better than his custom, whereupon, a waggish
friend present, knowing McComber's talent, suggested that he
should make a verse in honor of the new house, and the pro-
prietor should give him a dinner. The landlord, having no ob-
jection to a poetical compliment upon his stand, consented to the
arrangement; but demanded the verse before dinner. The poet
claimed the dinner first. At length they compromised, half the
verse before dinner, and the other half after, and McComber at
once recited,

> There swings a sign—'tis made of pine,
> And hangs among the trees;

Adjourning the completion till he had devoured the waiting dinner, with a facetious smile, he readily repeated and concluded,

> There swings a sign—'tis made of pine,
> And hangs among the trees;
> This house was once a house of prayer,
> But now a den of thieves.

Her husband being absent, Mrs. Mary Lamb was left, with the children, to take charge of the domestic affairs. One morning she heard a terrific scream in the dooryard, and on looking out saw a catamount making an onslaught upon the poultry. On opening the door the dog rushed out, and a fearful encounter followed. The dog finding himself unable to grapple successfully with his antagonist, fled into the house, followed by the catamount. Fear for the safety of the terrified children nerved the strong arm of the mother to desperation, and seizing the fire poker, she gave the "varmint" a heavy, well-directed blow, and with the assistance of the dog, now weak from loss of blood, succeeded in killing him. The dog died soon after, from wounds received in the contest. *Granville Addison Co. Vol. 1*

In September, Mrs. John Strong, whilst her husband and a few neighbors had joined together and gone up the lake in a bateau, and thence to Albany, to procure necessaries, one evening was sitting by the fire with her children about her. The evenings had become somewhat chilly. The kettle of samp intended for supper had just been taken from the fire, when, hearing a noise, she looked towards the door, and saw the blanket that served the purpose of one, raised up, and an old bear protruding her head into the room. The sight of the fire caused her to dodge back. *Addison Addison Co. Vol. 1*

Mrs. Strong caught the baby, and sending the older children to the loft, she followed and drew the ladder after her. The floor of this loft was made by lying small poles close together, which gave ample opportunity to see all passing below.

The bear, after reconnoitring the place several times, came in with two cubs. They first upset the milk that had been placed on the table for supper. The old bear then made a dash at the pudding-pot, and thrusting in her head, swallowed a large mouthful and filled her mouth with another before she found it was boiling hot. Giving a furious growl she struck the pot with her paw, upsetting and breaking it. She then set herself up on end, endeavoring to poke the pudding from her mouth, whining and growling all the time. This was so ludicrous, the cubs setting up on end, one on each side, and wondering what ailed their mother, that it drew a loud laugh from the children above.

This seemed to excite the anger of the beast more than ever, and with a roar she rushed for the place where they had escaped, up aloft. This they had covered up when they drew up the ladder, and now commenced a struggle; the bear to get up, the mother and children to keep her down. After many fruitless attempts, the bear gave it up, and towards morning moved off. After Strong's return, a door made from the slabs split from the basswood and hung on wooden hinges gave them some security from like inroads in future.

Charleston Abner Allyn has said that he has traveled back and forth on horse-
Orleans Co. back, carrying to and from home the necessaries for existence
Vol. III when his horse's legs sank so deep in the mud, that his own feet touched the ground, and that so heavy was the mud as to cause suction strong enough to actually draw the shoe from the horse's foot. He said at one time he alighted, took off his coat, raised his sleeve to his shoulder, thrust in his hand and arm above his elbow, grasped the horse-shoe, drew it up and carried it to be re-set at the nearest blacksmith-shop.

He related that at another time there was a heavy rain which beat into his log-house and put out all their fire. As the flint was their only way to strike fire, he often resorted to that; but unfortunately he had lent his gun to some hunters to be gone for days; so there was no other alternative than to leave his family in bed to keep from freezing, while he went to his neighbor, Judge Strong's, 4½ miles away to borrow fire. He did not like to tell of his calamity, so he asked to borrow the Judge's gun—returned with it, and struck fire, by which time wife and children were glad enough to rise.

At one time this family awoke in the night and found their house on fire. They had no modern fire-department, or even neighbors to call; so they managed as best they could. They carried a bed out of doors, put the children snugly into it, tucking up the bed-clothes well, to prevent them from getting out into the deep snow—then they went to work and took the entire roof off from the house; thus saving the rest of the house and its contents. Mr. Allyn was then obliged to take his team and go through the deep snows 12 miles to Barton, to draw boards with which to cover his house.

What a lonely spot this wilderness must have been for those youthful pioneers, ere a human foot had marked the soil, or the woodman's axe had once been heard! How full of hope and joy those sturdy men must have felt, as around them stood in this dense woods a few of their empty huts of logs, made by their own hands, into which they were about to introduce their youthful wives, as mistresses of such splendid palaces! With what a bounding heart James Lyon leaves the rude house of his toil for the fair hand of her who had promised to be his wife! It is almost idle to attempt to follow his hopeful steps as he leads his loving bride through the woods and over the hills of Strafford, following a line of marked trees, until, at last, tired and almost disheartened, *Tunbridge Orange Co. Vol. II*

they come to a pile of rough logs covered with bark—hear him
as he whispers in her ear, "My dear wife, this is the house that
James built; this is *our home!*" "O! How nice!" I imagine she ex-
claims; "there is no place like home!"

THOMAS PICKENS

Randolph used to get his fire-wood from a steep hill back of his house, let-
Orange Co. ting one log at a time slide down through the snow. One day a
Vol. II large log not following the track, struck the house and went
crashing through, under the oven, into the kitchen, where his
wife was busily engaged with her spinning-wheel; and although
she was a very small woman, and some startled, she neither had
fits, nor cried over it.

Randolph Mr. Tracy was the first teacher in the new school-house. He used,
Orange Co. when the mornings were cold, to take pudding and milk for his
Vol. II breakfast, and start as soon as it was light, so as to make a fire,
that the room might be comfortable when the children arrived.
There was a huge fire-place on one side of the room, and it was
rather a slow process to get the room warmed (the wood being
green) unless the fire was started betimes.

One morning, just as the sun was shedding a yellow light from
the east, Mr. Tracy neared his school-house. He noticed the door
was ajar, but thought some of the boys were in advance of him,
and pushing the door open, stood face to face with a huge bear,
and two half-grown cubs. Here was a dilemma; but he sprang to
the fire-place and caught a large shovel, which belonged to Mr.
Flint, and commenced a regular fight. He found that he had
nothing to fear from the cubs, as they only growled and showed
their teeth. It was getting pretty warm work, when Diah Flint

arrived, and, having a gun with him, soon dispatched the old bear and cubs, and then went for help to dress them, and by nine o'clock they had them all skinned and dressed; and as each team arrived with its load of scholars, the two young men introduced the learned animals to their notice, and the whole district rejoiced in a fine feast of bear meat for their suppers.

After the building was completed, and had been in use several years, it was suggested that it would be expedient to have it painted, and a lightning-rod put up, to ensure its safety. Dea. Flint said he was willing to have it painted, as he wished the Lord's house to look as respectable as his own, and he would assist in having it done; "but," said he, "I will never give a cent for a lightning rod; for, after we have built the Lord a house, if he chooses to set fire to it and burn it down, he can do it. I shall never object to his doing as he pleases with his own." This Baptist meeting-house was, in later years, converted into a hog-house, and still stands, used for that purpose, by Mr. Ketchum who owns the James Flint homestead.

Randolph Orange Co. Vol. II

The Indians who enacted the Royalton raid, to use an expression now much in vogue, seem to have possessed, with their savage propensities, quite a spice of humor, which, on several occasions they indulged with much apparent gusto. Among instances of this kind a ludicrous story has been handed down respecting their doings in Randolph.

Randolph Orange Co. Vol. II

On the banks of the Second Branch, within the borders of that town, along up which they passed on their retreat to Canada, there lived at the time a settler, whose family consisted of himself, his wife and his dog—the latter, as it would seem, occupying the first place in his affections; for the wife, if she was not sadly belied, was not only a great, fat, blousy, disagreeable creature, but a most intolerable slattern.

When the Indians were approaching, the man was standing some distance from his house near the borders of the woods. Attracted by suspicious sounds, he ran to a little elevation near by for a better view; when, to his dismay he beheld the whole gang of plunderers making their way rapidly towards his house. After glancing a moment towards the house where his unsuspecting wife was still remaining, and then stealing another hurried glance at the enemy, he seized his dog by the collar and drew him into the woods, where he selected a covert, from which, unseen, he peered out and awaited the result, still holding on to the dog to prevent him from barking or running out into view, so as to attract the notice of the Indians.

Presently the hostile party came up and entered the house. "Now, old woman, I guess you are gone for it," he said to himself, expecting every moment to hear her outcries under the tomahawk or scalping-knife, or see her brought out bound to be carried off as a prisoner. But he beheld neither: in a few moments he saw the Indians lead his wife out, and with mock gravity conduct her down to the stream into which they soused her up and down till they appeared to think she was sufficiently washed to be as clean as other folks. They then turned her adrift to mend her wet plight as she best could, but would not suffer her to go into the house; for, after taking from it such articles as they wanted, they consigned it to the flames, and departed on their way.

Newbury 1770. This whole section from Lancaster, N.H., to Northfield,
Orange Co. Mass., was smitten by a plague of worms. The inhabitants call
Vol. II them the "Northern Army," as they moved from the north and west to the east and south. It is affirmed that the Rev. Dr. Burton, of Thetford, said he had seen whole pastures so covered he could not put down his finger in a single spot without placing it upon

a worm, and that he had seen more than 10 bushels in a heap. They were sometimes found "not larger than a pin, but in their maturity were as long as a man's finger and proportionately large." "There was a stripe upon the back like black velvet, and on either side a yellow stripe, and they appeared to be in great haste except when they halted for food." "They did not take hold of the pumpkin vine, peas, potatoes, or flax, but wheat and corn disappeared before them." "They would climb up the stalks of wheat, eat off the stalk just below the head and almost as soon as the head had fallen upon the ground, it was devoured."

The men tried to save their wheat by a process called "drawing the rope." Two men would take a rope, one at each end, would pass through their wheat-fields and brush the worms from the stalk, but nothing could save it. There were fields of corn in Newbury so tall and luxuriant "it was difficult to see a man standing in the field more than one rod from the outermost row, that in ten days after the appearance of the worms, nothing but bare stalks remained." In vain the farmers dug trenches round their fields; they soon filled the ditch and the millions that pressed over on the backs of their fellows made a speedy destruction of the interdicted field.

Then the farmers dug trenches as before, but took sharpened stakes, of 6 or 8 inches in diameter and 6 or 8 feet in length, and drove them into the bottom of the ditch, once in 2 or 3 feet, and as these meadows were bottom-lands, easily made holes 2 to 3 feet in depth below the bottom of the trench. As the sides of the holes thus made were smooth, as soon as the worm stepped from, or was thrust over the brink, he fell to the bottom, and the destroyer coming round when the hole was pretty well filled, thrust in his pointed stick and made an extermination of every one. In this way a part of the farmers saved enough seed for the next year. About the first of September the worms suddenly disappeared, and not a worm or the skin of a worm was seen till in the Summer of 1781, when they appeared just 11 years afterward, the same kind of worm, but comparatively few in number.

Rockingham John Kilburn's house which partook somewhat of the nature of
Windham Co. a fort without being one, was nearly two miles further north,
Vol. V located on the low terrace. A desperate Indian fight occurred here
Aug. 17, 1755. Four hundred Indians demanded of Kilburn that
he and his party should surrender. But, although his force, all told,
consisted of but four men and two women, he indignantly refused
to surrender, and in reply to the chief who promised "good
quarter," he replied, "Begone, you black rascal, or I'll quarter
you!"

The fight immediately commenced. The Indians fired on the
house from the high terrace on the east, and the roof was soon
completely riddled. The women worked with a will loading the
guns, of which they had a number, and casting bullets. They
melted up their pewter spoons and dishes, and when these were
exhausted they suspended blankets in the chamber to catch the
Indian balls which were sent back with deadly effect into the
savage ranks. The unequal contest continued all the afternoon till
nearly dark, when the Indians, thinking that Kilburn must have
a regiment of men in the house, gave up the fight and returned
to Canada, and never dared to molest Walpole again.

Dummerston One common article of food was bean-porridge. It was eaten for
Windham Co. breakfast and, oftentimes, for supper. Dinner, usually, consisted
Vol. V of boiled meat and some kind of vegetables, most frequently
turnip. These were boiled in a large iron pot or kettle.

To make bean-porridge, a sufficient quantity of beans were
boiled with meat and turnip. When these were removed, the
residue with the beans, was made into porridge. In cold weather
enough was made at once to last several days.

Pumpkins were baked in the same way as bread, and also furnished a common article of food. A ripe pumpkin, having a very hard shell was taken, and a hole was cut in the stem-end some five or six inches in diameter, the piece being kept whole which was taken out. The seeds and all the stringy substance were then scraped out clean. Thus prepared, it was partly filled with new milk and covered with the piece taken out, placed in a well-heated oven and left to bake six or eight hours. It was allowed to cool in the oven, and, when served, was eaten with milk. Some scraped out the pumpkin and ate it in bowls—others turned the milk into the pumpkins and ate from the pumpkins.

It is granted that cold water was used when nothing stronger could be obtained; but strong drinks were much used, and the grandfathers were full of expedients to make them. Malt beer was a common beverage.

> "If barley be wanting to make into malt,
> We must then be contented, and think it
> no fault;
> For we can make liquor, to sweeten our lips
> Of pumpkins, and parsnips, and walnut tree
> chips."

From the settlings in beer-barrels, our grandmothers made "emptyings," a kind of yeast, so called because the barrels were emptied for the settlings.

Flip, a strong drink, was usually made of beer heated foaming hot with a red hot "loggerhead," and then pouring in a glass of rum. Punch was also a common drink and was passed round to the company in bowls. This kind of drink was so called because it originally contained five ingredients—water, sugar, tea, lemons, and arrack, a kind of spirit. The word means five. Later rum was the kind of spirit used, and milk was added to make milk-punch.

Black-strap was a cheap kind of drink and was drank when nothing better could be afforded. It was made of rum sweetened with molasses. Toddy and eggnogg furnished other varieties of drink. As soon as the people obtained orchards, cider was drank in large quantities by all classes, rich and poor. Hop-beer was also brewed and drank in large quantities. All drinking of the common people was social, all drinking from the same mug or bowl.

Dummerston Windham Co. Vol. V   Although the children of Lt. Leonard Spaulding, especially the sons, became large, muscular persons, all but one or two died under 40 years of age of consumption, and their sickness was brief.

It is related by those who remember the circumstance; after six or seven of the family had died of consumption, another daughter was taken, it was supposed, with the same disease. It was thought she would die, and much was said in regard to so many of the family's dying of consumption when they all seemed to have the appearance of good health and long life. Among the superstitions of those days, we find it was said that a vine or root of some kind grew from coffin to coffin, of those of one family, who died of consumption, and were buried side by side; and when the growing vine had reached the coffin of the last one buried, another one of the family would die; the only way to destroy the influence or effect, was to break the vine; take up the body of the last one buried and burn the vitals, which would be an effectual remedy: Accordingly, the body of the last one buried was dug up and the vitals taken out and burned, and the daughter, it is affirmed, got well and lived many years. The act, doubtless, raised her mind from a state of despondency to hopefulness.

Dummerston Windham Co. Vol. V   The eldest daughter of Capt. John and Martha Moore Kathan, was born, Oct. 6, 1730, probably in Worcester, Mass. She was married to Benjamin Moore, son of Capt. Fairbank Moore, May 11, 1755, and in less than three years after was taken prisoner by the Indians who broke into the house of Capt. Moore, her father-in-law, with whom she and her husband resided, at midnight Mar. 6, 1758, and killed her husband and the Captain, his father. She, startled from sleep by the terrible war-whoop of the savages, sprang from her bed and while the fierce attack was going on below, hurridly dressing herself and her children escaped from the house. It was in the middle of the night, dark and cold. Not knowing what she did in her fright she had pulled on in dressing two pair of long woolen stockings that proved of good service now and it probably saved her life. She took a sled-road for the woods, that her husband had broke the day before to draw wood.

With her two children, the youngest a babe of but three weeks old, she was soon overtaken by the Indians, who as soon as it was light discovered her footsteps in the snow. They took both of her children from her at first but soon returned her babe to her which they allowed her to carry; and they led or carried the oldest child that was but little over two years old. During the night the Indians finding in the house some beans and tallow, cooked the beans in about 20 pounds of tallow and put them up in bags for provision on the way; upon this they subsisted, traveling on foot to Fort Ticonderoga, which they reached on the tenth day from their departure; having crossed the Green Mountains in the most inclement season of the year; and from Ticonderoga they were taken by boat to Montreal in Canada, where Mrs. Moore and her children remained in captivity for two and a half years; her father's family in Dummerston, not knowing her fate till she was returned to them; Col. Peter Schuyler having "paid a ransom of four hundred livres ($74) for her redemption from captivity."

She came back to her friends in 1762.

SETH HUBBELL.

In the latter part of February, 1789, I set out from the town of Norwalk, in Connecticut, on my journey for Wolcott to com- *Wolcott Lamoille Co. Vol. II* mence a settlement; family consisting of my wife and five children, they all being girls, the eldest nine or ten years old. My team was a yoke of oxen and a horse. After I had proceeded on my journey to within about one hundred miles of Wolcott, one of my oxen failed, but I however kept him yoked with the other till about noon each day; then turned him before, and took his end of the yoke myself, and proceeded on in that manner with my load to about fourteen miles of my journey's end, when I could get the sick ox no further, and was forced to leave him with Thomas W. Connel, in Johnson; but he had neither hay nor grain for him.

I then proceeded on with some help to Esq. McDaniel's in Hydepark: this brought me to about eight miles of Wolcott, and to the end of the road. It was now about the 20th of March; the snow not far from four feet deep; no hay to be had for my team, and no way for them to subsist but by browse. As my sick ox at McConnel's could not be kept on browse, I interceded with a man in Cambridge for a little hay to keep him alive which I backed, a bundle at a time, five miles, for about ten days, when the ox died.

On the 6th of April I set out from Esq. McDaniel's his being the last house for my intended residence in Wolcott, with my wife and two oldest children. We had eight miles to travel on snow-shoes, by marked trees—no road being cut: my wife had to try this new mode of traveling and she performed the journey remarkably well. The path had been so trodden by snow-shoes as to bear up the children. To the east of us it was eighteen miles to inhabitants, and no road but marked trees; to the south, about twenty, where there was infant settlements, but no communication with us and 8 to the north, it was almost indefinite, or to the regions of Canada.

I had now got to the end of my journey, and I may say almost to the end of my property, for I had not a mouthfull of meat or kernel of grain for my family, nor had I a cent of money to buy with, or property that I could apply to that purpose. I however had the good luck to catch a sable. The skin I carried fifty miles,

and exchanged for half a bushel of wheat, and backed it home.

We had now lived three weeks without bread; though in the time I had bought a moose of an Indian, and backed the meat five miles, which answered to subsist upon. I would here remark that it was my fate to move on my family at that memorable time called the "scarce season," which was generally felt through the state, especially in the northern parts in the infant settlements: no grain or provision of any kind, of consequence, was to be had on the river Lamoile. I had to go into New Hampshire, sixty miles, for the little I had for my family, till harvest, and this was so scanty a pitance that we were under the painful necessity of allowancing the children till we had a supply. The three remaining children that I left in Hydepark, I brought, one at a time, on my back on snowshoes, as also the whole of my goods.

I moved from Connecticut with the expectation of having fifty acres of land given me when I came on, but this I was disappointed of, and was under the necessity soon after I came on of selling a yoke of oxen and a horse to buy the land I now live on which reduced my stock to but one cow; and this I had the misfortune to lose the next winter. But in the fall I had the good fortune to purchase another cow; but my misfortunes still continued, for in the June following she was killed by a singular accident. Again I was left without a cow, and here I was again frustrated in my calculations; this last cow left a fine heifer calf that in the next fall I lost by being choked.

Here I was left destitute—no money to buy, or article to traffic for one: but there was a door opened. I was informed that a merchant in Haverhill was buying snakeroot and sicily. This was a new kind of traffic that I had no great faith in; but I thought to improve every means or semblance of means in my power. Accordingly, with the help of my two oldest girls, I dug and dried a horseload, and carried this new commodity to the merchant; but this was like most hearsay, reports of fine markets, always a little way ahead, for he knew nothing about this strange article, and would not even venture to make me an offer; but after a long conference I importuned with the good merchant to give me a three year old heifer for my roots on certain conditions too tedious to mention. I drove her home and with joy she was welcomed to my habitation.

When I came into Wolcott, my farming tools consisted of one ax and an old hoe. The first year I cleared about two acres, wholly without any team, and being short of provision was obliged to work the chief of the time till harvest with scarce a sufficiency to support nature. My work was chiefly by the river. When too faint to labor, for want of food, I used to take a fish from the river, broil it on the coals, and eat it without bread or salt, and then to my work again. This was my common practice the first year till harvest. I could not get a single potato to plant the first season, so scarce was this article. I planted that which I cleared in season with corn; and an early frost ruined the crop, so that I raised nothing the first year: had again to buy my provision. My seed corn, about eight quarts cost me two and a half yards of whitened linen, yard wide, and this I had to go twenty miles after. After I raised a sufficiency for my family, I had to carry it twelve miles to mill on my back, for the three first years: this I had constantly to do once a week. My common load was one bushel, and generally carried it eight miles before I stopped to rest. My family necessities once obliged me to carry a moose hide thirty miles on my back, and sell it for a bushel of corn, and bring that home in the same way.

My scanty supply of bread-corn made it necessary to improve the first fruits of harvest of Lake Champlain to alleviate our distress, it being earlier than with us. Accordingly, on the last of July or the first of August, I took my sickle and set out for the Lake, a distance of better than forty miles. When I had got there, I found their grain was not ripe enough to begin upon; but was informed that on the Grand Isle they had begun their harvest. I was determined to go on, but had nothing to pay my passage. I finally hired a man to carry me over from Georgia for the small compensation of a case and two lances that I happened to have with me; but when I had got on to the Island, I found I was still too early. There was no grain ripe here, but I found the most forward I could, plead my necessity, and stayed by the owner till I got one and a half bushel of wheat, and worked for him to pay for it: it was quite green; I dried it and set out for home; but my haste to get back prevented my drying it sufficiently. I found a boat bound for Mansfield's mills, on the river Lamoille, and got my grain on board, and had it brought there free from expense. I got it ground or rather mashed, for it was too damp to make meal. I here hired my meal carried on to Cambridge borough for my sickle, and there got it ground the second time, but it was still far from good meal. From the borough I was so fortunate as to get it home on a horse. I was a fortnight on this tour.

A painful circumstance respecting my family I must here mention; In the year 1806 we were visited with sickness that was uncommonly distressing, five being taken down at the same time, and several dangerously ill. In this sickness I lost my wife, the partner of my darkest days, who bore her share of our misfortunes with becoming fortitude. I also lost a daughter at the same time, and another was bedrid about six months, and unable to perform the least labour for more than a year. This grievous calamity involved me in debts that terminated in the loss of my farm, my little all; but by the indulgence of feeling relatives I am still permitted to stay on it. Though I have been doomed to hard fortune I have been blest with a numerous offspring; have had by my two wives seventeen children, thirteen of them daughters; have had forty-seven grand-children, and six great grand-children, making my posterity seventy souls.

When I reflect on those past events, the fatigue and toil I had to encounter, the dark scenes I had to pass through, I am struck with wonder and astonishment at the fortitude and presence of mind that I then had to bear me up under them. Not once was I discouraged or disheartened; I exercised all my powers of body and mind to do the best I could, and left the effect for future events to decide, without embarrassing my mind with imaginary evils. I could lay down at night, forgetting my troubles, and sleep composed and calm as a child; I did in reality experience the just proverb of the wise man, that "the sleep of the laboring man is sweet, whether he eat little or much."

2

The Revolutionary Era,
1776 to 1791

Violence against New Yorkers broke out at Cumberland County Court in Windsor, 1771 : Ethan Allen and his Green Mountain Boys harassed New York land-title holders : Westminster Massacre in March 1775, in a revolt against New York sovereignty : In May 1775, Ethan Allen and eighty-three followers captured sleepy British garrison at Fort Ticonderoga, New York : Vermont became an independent republic, July 8, 1777 : In Hubbardton on July 7, 1777, occurred the only revolutionary battle fought on Vermont soil : Battles of Bennington and Saratoga, which followed, secured the northern frontier for insurgent colonists : Vermont joined the Union as the fourteenth state March 4, 1791.

"THE HAMPSHIRE GRANTS in particular, a country unpeopled and almost unknown in the last war, now abounds in the most active and rebellious race on the continent, and hangs like a gathering storm on my left." General Burgoyne to Lord Germain, August 20, 1777. *Danby Rutland Co. Vol. III*

LIEUT. BENJAMIN EVEREST

Addison
Addison Co.
Vol. 1
was born in Seabury, Conn., and moved with his father to
Addison when sixteen years of age. This was in 1769. In August,
1773, when Allen, Warner, and Baker came up to help the settlers
drive off Col. Reid and his Yorkers from their position at
Vergennes, Everest with his brother Zadock and other neighbors
joined them. After having torn down the mills, burned the dwellings, and destroyed the settlement, and being all ready to return,
Allen made such an impression on Benjamin, their spirits were so
much in unison, that Everest wished to go with Allen, as more
trouble with the Yorkers was expected. Allen was glad of his
service, and very soon gave him a sergeant's warrant in his band.
From this time until the opening of the Revolution he was with
Allen more or less.

On receipt of intelligence of the battle of Lexington, Everest
immediately repaired to Allen's head-quarters, where he received
a commission as Lieutenant, which was afterwards confirmed. He
was very active and useful in procuring men and information to
aid in the capture of Ticonderoga and Crown Point, and was with
Allen when he entered the fort of Ticonderoga, and went up with
Warner to take Crown Point. After Allen was taken prisoner at
Montreal, Everest and his company was incorporated into Col.
Seth Warner's regiment. He was with Warner at the battle of
Hubbardton, and with his company as rangers held the British in
check by skirmishing in the woods from point to point, facilitat-
ing and covering the retreat of Warner. Warner was not at Bennington at the commencement of the battle, but having information from Stark of the approach of Baum, with orders to hasten
to his aid, he did so, and arrived just at the most critical time. Col.
Breymen, who had been sent to Baum's relief, arrived on the
ground. Soon after Warner arrived, and at a glance saw the peril
of our troops, and gave the word to "Close!" when, like an eagle
swooping to its prey, so he and his Green Mountain Boys came

down on the enemy, and scattered them like dust before the wind. Night closing in favored the escape of the enemy, but they lost 207 killed and about 700 prisoners. After the capture of Burgoyne, Everest obtained a furlough, with the intention of visiting Addison to look after his father's property—his father having gone back to Connecticut with his family.

When living in this town, during the troublesome times with the "Yorkers," Lt. John Wyman was very active in maintaining the rights of inhabitants to claims of land purchased from the Governor of New Hampshire. The government of New York declared the titles of the land grants good for nothing, and required the occupants to purchase the lands a second time. Many refused to do this; their lands were sold to other persons; and the holders were sued and ordered to leave. They would not do it; and roughly handled the sheriffs and others, who attempted to force them away. The people at length became so enraged that they would not allow any person who sympathized with the Yorkers to remain at liberty, but arrested all such persons and put them in jail at Westminster. *Dummerston Windham Co. Vol. V*

Colonel Church, who lived in the edge of Brattleboro on the West River road, was a "Yorker" in political sentiment, and to punish him for entertaining such provocative opinions, the "committee of safety" were determined to "jug him." Lieut. Wyman and Charles Davenport were the leaders of the party that proceeded to the house of the Colonel for the purpose of taking him prisoner. On their arrival, Wyman knocked loudly for admittance but no one answered the call, and the door was found to be securely fastened. He shook, pounded and kicked at the door making a tremendous noise, when it opened suddenly and a dish of hot porridge was thrown into his face. This unexpected calamity did not hinder the proceedings—the men rushed in and searched the house thoroughly but could find nothing of the Colonel inside the building.

Mr. Davenport in the meantime had searched the barn and sheds but not finding him there; looked around the outside of the house. He soon found a small opening through the underpinning and crawled in to reconnoitre the grounds. It was a difficult passage; but he pushed on through the gloomy labyrinth of cobwebs till at last he spied the Colonel snugly tucked away in the remotest corner. Fearing he might have a gun with him, he ventured no farther, but crawled back, went into the house and, going directly over the place, he jumped violently on the floor, "There!" said he, "the Colonel is right under here." All rushed to the hole, and Davenport again crawled through, and crept cautiously towards him till he was satisfied he had no gun, then venturing quite near said, "Come out." He came out and was (later) safely lodged in jail.

Bradford The party feeling between the adherents to the New Hampshire
Orange Co. and the New York claims was never as strongly developed in this
Vol. II town as in some of the adjoining towns. The New Hampshire party always had the predominance in this town. Some little vexatious matters occasionally transpired. As an instance: A man by the name of Frazier was sued for debt from spite by a Yorker. His cows were attached and some other property, and his person was seized for imprisonment. As soon as the condition of Mr. Frazier was known, the alarm was given throughout the town, and the New Hampshire men rallied for his rescue. Joseph Williams seized a horn, and from the hill north of the place, afterwards occupied by Solomon Bascom, blew a blast that brought to the aid of Frazier the west part of the town, and some from Whitingham and Wilmington, who, with others already on the track, pursued the party who had taken Frazier to Westminster for imprisonment, and with the assistance of the company from Westmoreland, New Hampshire, succeeded in his rescue.

Bennington Battle-Grounds

On the 7th of February, 1775, a convention was held at West- *Westminster* minster, whose main object was to obtain, if possible, from the *Windham Co.* legislature of New York, the passage of such laws as would tend *Vol. V* to improve the mode of administering justice in the county courts. Their special cause of grievance was the "great expense and heavy burdens" imposed upon them by reason of the additional courts that had been established, in consequence of which, lawsuits had increased and charges had been multiplied and families nearly beggared.

The "acts and resolves" of the Continental Congress which had been adopted by the people of Cumberland county in open convention, had however been rejected by the General Assembly of New York. And while in the other colonies the meeting of the Continental Congress had been followed by an almost universal suspension of royal authority, the higher civil officers in the colony of New York remained loyal to the King, and the courts still continued to be held, but being administered in the interests of the crown they were so oppressive as to be almost insufferable on the part of those who had espoused the liberal cause. And those who expressed their dissatisfaction were denounced as "guilty of high treason," for withholding their allegiance from the King.

The people were no longer willing to trust themselves in the hands of those whom they regarded as enemies of American liberty. And "in duty to God, to themselves, and to their posterity, they thought themselves under the strongest obligations to resist and to oppose all authority that would not accede to the resolves of the Continental Congress."

Such was the state of feeling which led to that memorable event in the history of this town, known as:

The Westminster Massacre,

which occurred on the 13th of March, 1775. The scene of this

event was the "Old Court House," which stood at the extreme
north end of the Lower Street, on the east side of the road on the
spot now known as "Court House Hill," but a short distance from
the meeting-house which then occupied the middle of the highway. This building was erected in 1772, at which time the courts
of Cumberland county were removed from this place to Chester.

The courts were held there until 1781, when Westminster and
Marlborough became half shire towns, until 1787, when New
Fane became the county town and a new court-house and jail
were erected there. The old court-house in Westminster stood till
about the year 1806.

The 14th of March, 1775, was the day on which the county
court was to commence at Westminster. To avoid all rashness
and unnecessary collision with the Court party, it was thought
best to request the judges to remain at home. For this purpose
"about forty good, true men," went from Rockingham to Chester
to dissuade Col. Chandler, the chief judge, from attending court.
He "thought it would be for the good of the country not to hold
any court, as things were; but there was one case of murder that
they must see to, and if it was not agreeable to the people they
would not hear any other case." Someone said that "the sheriff
would raise a number of men, and there would be blood shed."
The judge assured them upon his word and honor that there
would be no arms brought against them.

Noah Sabin, one of the associate judges, "was very earnest to
have the law go on," as well as many petty officers. Col. Wells,
the other associate judge, was absent, in attendance upon the
General Assembly at New York.

There was much debate among the Whigs as to what means
they would adopt to prevent the sitting of the Court. It was at
length agreed to let the Court come together and then present
their reasons for not wishing it to proceed. But upon learning that
the Court was to take possession of the house on the 13th inst.,
and place a strong guard at the doors, they thought best to effect
an entrance "before the armed guards were placed," that they

might lay before the Court their grievances before it opened.

On Monday, March 13, a party of Whigs from Rockingham came down to Westminster and halted at the house of Capt. Azariah Wright, and repaired from thence to the school house on the opposite side of the street, and held consultation as to the best manner to prevent the sitting of the Court.

Having armed themselves with sticks from Capt. Wright's wood-pile, they proceeded on their way, and were joined by others armed like themselves, and on arriving at the court-house, the whole party, to the number of about one hundred, entered about 4 o'clock in the afternoon.

Soon after this, the High Sheriff, Wm. Paterson, who had on the day previous gone to Brattleborough to obtain assistance in preserving the peace, came up with a large number of men, some of them "armed with guns, swords and pistols, and others with sticks or clubs."

Approaching within about 5 yards of the door, the Sheriff commanded the "rioters," as they were called, to disperse, but obtained no answer. He then ordered the "King's proclamation" to be read, and told them, with an oath, if they did not disperse within fifteen minutes, he would "blow a lane through them." The Whigs replied, they would not disperse, but the Sheriff and his company might come in if they would lay aside their arms, but not without.

One of the party within advanced to the door and asked the Tories if they had "come for war," saying "we are come for peace, and would be glad to hold a parley with you." Whereupon Samuel Gale, Clerk of the Court, drew a pistol, and replied with an oath, he would hold no parley with them but by this—referring to his pistol.

The Tories then withdrew a short distance after some pretty harsh language, and held a consultation, and the Whigs sent out three men to treat with them, but with no avail.

About 7 o'clock Col. Chandler came in and they laid the case before him, reminding him of his promise that no arms should be brought against them. He said the arms were brought without his consent, but he would go and take them away, and they should enjoy the house undisturbed until morning, and that the Court should then come in without arms, and would hear what they had to lay before them. Having given them this assurance, he departed. The Whigs then left the house and chose a committee to draw up a list of articles to present to the Court, which was unanimously adopted by the company. Some of them then went home, and some to the neighbors, having left a guard at the court-house to give the alarm in case of an attack during the night.

Meanwhile, the sheriff had sent word to all the Tories in the neighborhood to come to his assistance. They met for consultation at Norton's Tavern, whence they proceeded in small parties to the court-house a little before midnight. Their approach was discovered by the sentry, who gave order to "man the doors."

The sheriff marched his company within about 10 rods of the court-house, and advancing towards the door, demanded entrance in His Majesty's name. Seeing his demand was not regarded he told them he should enter quietly if he could, or by force if he must. Being twice repulsed in attempting to effect an entrance, he then ordered his men to fire.

Three shots were fired which passed over the heads of those within. The order was then repeated and several men were wounded; one, Wm. French, was shot with five bullets, one of which passed through his brain, of which wound he died the next day.

"Then," we quote the words of an eye-witness, "they rushed in with their guns, swords, and clubs, and did most cruelly maim several more, and took some that were not wounded, and those that were, and crowded them all into close prison together, and then told them they should be in hell before the next night, and that they did wish that there were forty more in the same case with that dying man. When they put him into prison, they took and dragged him as one would a dog, and would mock him as he lay gasping, and make sport for themselves at his dying motions."

In this bloody affray, two of the sheriff's party received slight flesh wounds, and of the Whig party some escaped, ten were wounded, two of them mortally, and seven were taken prisoner.

Tuesday morning, the 14th, all was confusion. At the appointed hour the court convened and prepared a statement of the facts, "exactly as they happened," in the "very melancholy and unhappy affair," that had occurred during the night. It was thought best not to proceed with business, and an adjournment was made to the second Tuesday in June. That session has never been held.

Meanwhile messengers had been dispatched in all directions and the tidings quickly spread. By noon of the next day more than 400 persons had assembled at Westminster, about half of whom were from New Hampshire; Capt. Benjamin Bellows came with his company from Walpole, and Capt. Sargent with his from Rockingham, another with an organized band from Guilford, and the Westminster militia were in full force under Capt. Azariah Wright.

The prisoners who had been confined the night previous were soon set at liberty, and before night the judges with their assistants, the sheriff and such of his party as were engaged in the massacre as could be taken, were put under arrest.

It was with difficulty that the enraged populace were restrained from doing acts of violence. Some demanded that the judges should be brought forth and make satisfactory acknowledgments; and some threatened to burn the court-house and shoot every man engaged in the massacre of the previous night. Through the influence of Capt. Bellows they were dissuaded from carrying their threats into execution.

The morning of the 15th witnessed a renewal of the scenes of the preceding day. An inquest was held on the body of young French, and the sheriff and those of his party imprisoned with him were placed in close confinement.

During the day reinforcements came from the southern part of the county and from the Massachusetts province, and from the west side of the Green Mountains, so that upon the morning of the 16th it was computed that there were "five hundred good martial soldiers, well equipped for war," assembled in West-minster, besides others who had come as private citizens.

A public meeting was held, and a large committee chosen, to consist of persons out of the county as well as in, who, "after the most critical and impartial examination of evidence," decided that the leaders in the massacre should be "confined in Northampton jail till they could have a fair trial," and those who appeared less guilty should be "under bonds, holden to answer at the next court of Oyer and Terminer" to be held in the county. Here they remained some two weeks, until they were removed on a writ of habeas corpus to New York, for a regular trial in order to their enlargement. We do not learn as they ever had their trial. The Revolutionary War had now become a fact, and other interests were absorbed in that.

WILLIAM FRENCH,

one of the victims of this massacre, was a son of Nathaniel French, who lived in Brattleborough, near the southern line of Dummerston. He was a young man of patriotic spirit, and an ardent sympathizer with the liberty party. He was one of those stationed in the court-house on that eventful night of the 13th of March, 1775, animated by that liberty loving spirit, whose smouldering fires were now ready to burst forth in a general uprising throughout the colonies. He fell pierced with five bullets in as many different places, one of which entered the brain just behind the ear, and caused his death.

Dr. Wm. Hill, of Westminster, was allowed to visit him between three and four the next morning, but his martyr spirit had fled.

Mr. French was buried the same day with military honors in the old graveyard at Westminster, and a stone with the following quaint inscription, marks the spot where he was laid:

In Memory of WILLIAM FRENCH.
Son to Mr. Nathaniel French. Who
Was Shot at Westminster March ye 13th,
1775, by the hands of Cruel Ministerial tools.
Of Georg ye 3d, in the Corthouse at a 11
a Clock
at Night in the 22nd year of his Age.

HERE WILLIAM FRENCH his Body lies.
For murder his Blood for Vengance cries
King Georg the third his Tory crew
tha with a Bawl his head Shot threw.
For Liberty and his Countrys Good.
he Lost his Life his Dearest blood.

Young French has been claimed by historians as the first martyr whose blood was shed in the cause of the American Revolution. This claim, however, has been disputed, but upon how good authority we are not able to say. An attempt was made in 1852, by some of the most distinguished and patriotic citizens of Vermont, to obtain from the Legislature an appropriation for the purpose of erecting a monument to his memory. The bill was, however, defeated by a small majority. When Vermont, in 1877, met at Westminster to celebrate the One Hundredth Anniversary of the declaration of her independence as a State, measures were taken for the erection of a monument in honor of her first blood shed in the cause of American liberty, upon that sacred spot where that first blood was shed and where her independence was declared.

An incident relating to John Kathan, Jr., is given in Hall's History. In 1779, he refused to serve in the Vermont militia. June 17 of that year, John Kathan and Benjamin Jones, Jr., both of Dummerston, were informed by an officer that they were required to

Dummerston Windham Co. Vol. V

do military duty. On their refusal to comply, being subjects of New York, the officer took a cow from each and sold one of them at auction, and retained the other for the use of the state. Ezra Robinson and Ephraim Rice, also, of this town had cattle sold in the same manner because they refused to pay or serve in the militia.

Bennington
Bennington Co.
Vol. I

The early importance of the town in the state organization is shown by the fact that of the provision tax assessed by the legislature in October, 1780, for supplying the troops of the state for the next year, more than one-fourteenth part was levied upon Bennington. So of a body of 300 men raised for permanent service in 1782, twenty-four—more than one-thirteenth of the whole were furnished by this town. It may be here mentioned that the provision tax for Bennington in 1780, consisted of 82 barrels of flour, 26 of Beef, 13 of Pork, 413 bushels of corn, and 206 bushels of rye, and that was merely for victualling the troops, leaving the cost of transportation, the munitions of war and the monthly pay of the officers and men to be otherwise provided for.

THE DUMMERSTON YORKER,

Dummerston
Windham Co.
Vol. V

Alexander Kathan, was in the fight on the side of the Court party, or "Tories" as they were called; and so indignant were the citizens towards him, that he was arrested and sentenced to remain on his farm one year, and not step off from it under penalty of death. A neighbor on the farm joining his, watched him daily during the whole year and always kept a loaded gun with him while at work in the field, for the purpose of shooting him the moment that he should step over the boundary. "It was lucky for him," said the man, "that he strictly kept within his limit, for I should have shot him as quick as I would an Indian."

JOHN JACOB PEELER

died March 24, 1815, in his 70th year. He enlisted in the British *Vernon* army for 5 years. He and two others left the fort commanded by *Windham Co.* Gen. Campbell without receiving their discharge were pursued *Vol. V* by John Hare, captured, brought back, tried by court martial, and sentenced, each, to receive 999 lashes upon the naked back, with a cat-o-nine tails, and after a blow the lashes were straightened before another was given.

One of the three died before he had received the complement and the rest were inflicted afterward, the other died three days after his chastisement.

Mr. Peeler said he should have died, if he had not crawled from the bunk around the floor. His comrade said he could not do it. Mr. Peeler told them he should desert when he recovered, and when he was sent to a swamp with a bog-hoe, he left again and was not again found. He then enlisted in the American army in the Revolutionary War. At the battle of Bunker Hill, he took a powder-horn from a British soldier, which is now in the possession of A. H. Washburn. His daughter said his back was one solid scar.

In the year 1781, the town of Shaftsbury received an order from *Shaftsbury* Col. Herrick for 31 men to serve as militia men or soldiers for the *Bennington Co.* ensuing campaign; a meeting of the town was called at which *Vol. I* Gideon Olin presided as Moderator, when the following business was transacted, to wit:

"*1st*. Voted, unanimously to raise a bounty and our quota of State troops for the ensuing campaign on the list of the polls and ratable estate of the town.——*2nd*. Voted to repose, and do hereby repose the trust of enlisting our quota of troops for this campaign in the hands of Capt. Wm. Dyer, Capt. Jonas Galusha,

Capt. B. Lawrence and Lieut. David Galusha, and to allow one dollar in hard money for enlisting each man.——*3rd*. Voted to give Mr. John Olin and Peter Mattison twenty shillings each for collecting said tax in the compass of Capt. Galusha's company, and David Cutter thirty shillings for collecting in the bounds of Capt. Lawrence's company, and they are hereby appointed for said purpose.——*4th*. Voted to give twenty dollars to each soldier, in hard money or continental, at the current exchange, to be raised forthwith for the above purpose."

At another meeting of the town in the same year, an animated debate was held regarding a previous tax, and the following was the conclusion by vote:

"That each man shall be taxed his equal proportion according to his List, of the beef, pork, flour, corn and rye to be assessed. The meat to be delivered at Capt. Waldo's, the flour and grain at Capt. Galusha's, innkeeper;" "and 87 bushels of wheat to be granted by town for the purpose of purchasing salt and barrels."

Bridport Addison Co. Vol. I The war of the Revolution commenced. A Tory—who was a tenant in the house of a Mr. Prindle—set fire to the house and left, implicating Mr. Stone in the robbery and burning. Mr. Stone, anticipating mischief, secreted himself among the bushes on the bank near his house, where he was discovered by the British, who fired upon him; but the volley of grape-shot struck among the trees above him. They also fired upon his house, and some of the balls entered the room where his family were. They then sent a boat on shore, captured Mr. Stone, and took him to Ticonderoga, where he remained three weeks.

Mrs. Stone, expecting he would be sent to Quebec, that she might again see her husband before his departure, shut up her two little children alone in their cabin, bidding the elder, which was but four years of age, to take good care of the baby till mother came back, who was going to take poor papa his clothes, went in a canoe to carry them, a distance of 12 miles, accompanied only by her brother, a lad of ten years. After she arrived, in order to gain admittance to her husband she must remain over night. The mother thought of her babe; alone in the cottage in the woods through all the long night; but could she turn from the door of her husband's prison, and perhaps see him no more? No, her babes the tender mother commited, in her heart, to the Good Father, and tarried till the morning; and upon her return found her little children safe, the elder having understood enough of her directions to feed and take care of the younger.

Mrs. Jabez Penniman was the widow of Ethan Allen, and married to Dr. Penniman at Westminster, Vt., Oct. 28th, 1793. *Colchester Chittenden Co. Vol. 1*

She was a woman highly esteemed, of brilliant mind, and a highly cultivated taste; and possessed those qualifications that made her an agreeable companion. She took great delight in the management and cultivation of a garden—which she would stock with rare varieties of flowers. The cultivation and improvement of wild flowers attracted her attention; and she made the study of botany a favorite amusement. She was born April 4th, 1760, and was married to General Allen, at Westminster, on the 9th of February, 1784.

It is well understood, that she always exerted a very decided influence over her brave yet eccentric husband—so much so, that her advice and good admonitions were held by him in a sort of submissive yet manly reverence. She often gave him gentle reproof, and reminded him of his faults; and especially desired to reform him from the habit of being out late at night with dissipated company—to which he was inclined.

It is related of her, on one occasion, that she adopted a very ingenious method of restraining him in this matter. After having had a good time, she rebuked him in good earnest; and, instead of admitting the justice of her reproof, he expressed doubts as to the truth and correctness of her remarks. "I will find out," she says, "whether you come home drunk or sober:" and thereupon she drove a nail pretty well up in the wall of the bedroom, and said to him: "There, Ethan, when your watch is hanging on that nail in the morning, I shall know that you came home sober." "Agreed," says the old hero.

He, however, found it rather a difficult job to prove his good behavior at all times by this severe' test. When he had taken a drop too much, as many did in those days, he would make a dash at the nail, but it would dodge him, and the watch ring hit one side; but he would brave up his resolution and nerves and make another rally, and the floor would now give way, or perhaps his knees get out of joint; yet not discouraged, he would stick to it and work up to the nail, until he got the ring of his watch fairly hooked, when he would retire satisfied that all would be right with Fanny this time. If she had a word to say in the morning, he would point his finger to the watch, Fanny do you see that? I came home sober last night."

Cabot The famous "yellow house" was built by Horace and Gershom
Washington Co. Beardsley, two stirring settlers from Massachusetts. It was the
Vol. IV first framed house in town, and was first raised in the pasture now owned by Samuel S. Batchelder. At that time a new county was formed from towns set off from the County of Orange, and there was a strong prospect that this town would be the shire town of the new county. With this expectation, the Beardsleys cleared two acres of land in this pasture, taking out the stumps, root and branch, for the site of the county buildings. Their hopes not being realized, the house was not finished on this spot, and after standing here about 2 years, was taken down and removed to the Plain. The timber, all hard wood, and the house two stories, it took a large amount of help to raise it, of men and whisky.

All the men and women in this town, Peacham and Danville

were invited to the raising. Those invited giving out word that they would drink the Beardsleys dry that day, the Beardsleys prepared themselves. They furnished a barrel of first proof rum, and a second barrel, slightly reduced. It was said never was such rum seen in Cabot before or after. All were invited to take hold and help themselves. In after years the old settlers enjoyed rehearsing the scenes at that raising. They said with a great many of them it lasted two days.

After the removal of the house to the Plain it was nicely finished, and became the "hub" of the town. It was 40 feet square upon the ground, with a large hall in the ell, used for all kinds of gatherings, and had a long shed attached running to the barn. As all the travel from the north going to the Connecticut river had to pass over Cabot Plain, it was a favorite stopping-place for travelers, and during the war of 1812, those engaged in smuggling made it their quarters.

PERVERSION OF LEGAL MAXIMS.

By a strange perversion of legal principles, which prevailed among the early settlers of Windham County, it was supposed that whoever married a widow who was administratrix upon the estate of her deceased husband represented insolvent, and should thereby possess himself of any property or thing which had been purchased by the deceased husband, would become an *exécuteur de son tort*, and would thereby make himself liable to answer for the goods and estate of his predecessor. To avoid this difficulty, Major Moses Joy, of Putney, who became enamored of Mrs. Hannah Ward of Newfane, the widow of William Ward, who died about 1788 leaving an insolvent estate, of which Mrs. Ward was administratrix, and married her within three months after taking out letters of administration.

The marriage took place in the old Field Mansion on Newfane

Newfane Windham Co. Vol. V

Hill, February 22, A.D. 1789, and was solemnized by Rev. Hezekiah
Taylor. Mrs. Ward placed herself in a closet, with a tire-woman,
who stripped her of all her clothing, and while in a perfectly
nude state, she thrust her fair, round arm through a diamond hole
in the door of the closet, and the gallant major clasped the hand
of the widow, and was married in due form by the jolliest parson
in Vermont. At the close of the ceremony, the tire-woman
dressed the bride in a complete wardrobe which the major had
provided and caused to be deposited in the closet at the commencement of the ceremony. She came out elegantly dressed in
silk, satin and lace.

Grand Isle
Grand Isle Co.
Vol. II
Indian hemp was good for dropsy; spignet root for internal
bruises; the bark of red willow a sure remedy for fever and ague;
burdock root with black cherry and white ash-bark steeped in
cider, the very best remedy for Spring jaundice.

Grand Isle
Grand Isle Co.
Vol. II
Dr. Jacob Roebeck was—as memory paints him—a short, stout-
made man, large head, broad shoulders, short neck, and short
lower limbs, florid complexion, and blue eyes; extremely gar-
ralous when under the influence of liquor and sometimes a little
vulgar: when sober, he was sad-looking and taciturn.

To my question: "Doctor, if I am ever as learned and wise as
you are, must I drink so much rum?" How grave he looked, how
long he paused, then said, "No, no, my poy, don't drink rum;
rum ish pad for poys but very goot for old doctors." "Do all
doctors drink rum?" I asked. "Not the doctors in the colleges in
Germany; they drink wine and peer, but all the doctors in
Burgoyne's army did, all the doctors in this country, they *do*
drink rum if they can't get prandy. "Why," said he, "how could
I have gone through those long marches with Burgoyne; how

could I have gone with Baum through the hard fights at Hubbardton and Bennington, taking care of the wounded and dying, without rum in my canteen?"

Several families moved into Troy and Potton [across the border in   *Troy*
Quebec] in 1799, and in the winter of 1799 and 1800 a small   *Orleans Co.*
party of Indians, of whom the chief man was Capt. Susap, joined   *Vol. III*
the colonists, built their camps on the river, and wintered near
them. These Indians were represented as being in a necessitous and
almost starving condition, which probably arose from the moose
and deer (which formerly abounded here) being destroyed by
the settlers. Their principal employment was making baskets,
birch-bark cups and pails, and other Indian trinkets. They left in
the Spring and never returned.

One of these Indians, a woman called Molly Orcutt, exercised
her skill in a more dignified profession, and her introduction to
the whites was rather curious.

In the Fall or beginning of the Winter in 1799, one of the
settlers purchased and brought in a barrel of whiskey and two
half barrels of gin and brandy. The necessities of the people for
this opportune supply may be referred from the fact the whole
was drunk or sold and carried off within three days from its
arrival. The arrival of a barrel of liquor in the settlement was, at
that time, hailed with great demonstrations of joy, and there was
a general gathering at the opening of the casks. So it was on this
occasion, a large party from Troy, Potton, and even from Rich-
ford, were assembled for the customary carousal. Their orgies
were held in a new house, and were prolonged to a late hour of
the night.

A transient, a rowdy from abroad by the name of Perkins,
happened there at that time, and in the course of the night grew
insolent and insulting and a fight ensued between him and one
Norris of Potton. In the contest Norris fell, or was knocked into

a great fire that was burning in the huge Dutch-back chimney
which was in the room. Norris' hair and clothes were severely
scorched but the main injury he sustained was in one hand which
was badly burned. The flesh inside of the hand was burned, or
torn off by the fall, so that the cords were exposed. The injury
was so serious that it was feared he would lose the use of his hand.
A serious difficulty now arose; there was no doctor in the settlement, no pain extractors or other patent medicines had found
their way there, and no one in the valley had skill or confidence
enough to undertake the management of so difficult a case.

Molly Orcutt was known as an Indian doctress, and then resided some miles off, near the Lake. She was sent for, and came
and built her camp near by, and undertook the case, and the hand
was restored. Her medicine was an application of warm milk-
punch. Molly's fame as a doctress was now raised. The dysentery
broke out with violence that Winter, particularly among children,
and Molly's services were again solicited, and she again undertook
the work of mercy, and again she succeeded. But in this case
Molly maintained all the reserve and taciturnity of her race: she
retained the nature of her prescription to herself, she prepared
her nostrum in her own camp, and brought it in a coffee pot to
her patients, and refused to divulge the ingredients of her prescription to any one; but chance and gratitude drew it from her.

In the March following, as Mr. Josiah Elkins and his wife were
returning from Peacham, they met Molly at Arnold's mills in
Derby; she was on her way across the wilderness to the Connecticut River, where she said she had a daughter married to a
white man. Mr. Elkins inquired into her means of prosecuting
so long a journey through the forest and snows of Winter, and
found she was but scantily supplied with provisions, having nothing but a little bread. With his wonted generosity, Mr. Elkins immediately cut a slice of pork of 5 or 6 pounds out of the barrel
he was carrying home, and gave it to her. My informant remarks
she never saw a more grateful creature than Molly was on receiving this gift. "Now you have been so good to me," she ex-

claimed, "I will tell you how I cured the folks this Winter of the dysentery," and told him her receipt. It was nothing more nor less than a decoction of the inner bark of the spruce.

The late Widow Learnard, born in 1766, is thought to have been the first child born in town. Their nearest neighbor was Captain Pannel, who lived on Pannel hill four miles distant. Mr. Pratt had occasion to leave his wife and two small children at home in his absence of 10 days. The first or second night of his absence, the fire went out. Mrs. P. had no means of obtaining fire but from her neighbors. She took her two children, one in her arms, leading the other, and started for Captain Pannel's through a dense forest guided by marked trees. When she had gone a little distance from her home she roused a bear who ran up a tree. With self-possession she took her apron and tied it around the tree, and hanging her bonnet upon a stake she placed it against the tree and passed on. Captain Pannel returned with her and shot the bear, which had been kept upon the tree by the bonnet and apron. Those were days of female courage as well as hardship, inured as they were to life in the wilderness.

Halifax Windham Co. Vol. V

It is related in the [Noah Morse] family, that, while the still unbroken forest nearly surrounded the homestead, a daughter of this household, one moonless night, kept faithful vigil for an expected lover. The no less faithful lover was making good way up the steep hill which the house crowned, rapt, without question, in sweet musings of the kind welcome near. But let lovers in a wilderness ever keep one ear open. Suddenly, the stealthy tread of a wild beast kept pace close by the roadside, the darkness was too thick to readily discover the unwelcome attendant; all doubt was, however, quickly removed by the terrific scream of a panther. At a

Dorset Bennington Co. Vol. 1

single leap down the hillside the arrested lover put distance between him and his waiting Love; and such fear lent wings to his
flight he soon outstripped even the bounding catamount. A party
of hunters was soon on the track, following on to the Green
Mountains eastward, they found crouched on the top of a hemlock stub, some 40 feet from the ground a full-grown catamount
—found to measure 8 feet—which two balls dispatched. It was
easy, moreover, it may well be inferred, for a sensible girl to for-
give his not keeping troth that night; and not withstanding the
untoward event above narrated, the runaway lover became her
husband.

Rutland No man in Vermont surpassed the mulatto minister, Rev. Lemuel
Rutland Co. Haynes of West Rutland, in readiness of wit and sharpness of
Vol. III repartee. He was often put to the trial, but it never failed. Two
reckless young men once made an experiment, having agreed together for that purpose: "Father Haynes," said one of them, "have
you heard the good news?" "No," said Haynes, "what is it?" "It
is great news indeed," said the other, "and if it is true, your business is at an end." "What is it?" repeated Mr. Haynes. "Why,"
said the first, "the devil is dead!" Lifting up his hands, and placing
one upon the head of each young man, he repeated, in a tone of
deep concern, "Oh! poor fatherless children! what *will* become
of you!"

   He went one evening into a store where liquor was drank, as
well as sold. In his pleasant manner he addressed the company,
"How d' ye do? How do you all do here?" The merchant, willing
to joke a little, replied, "Oh, not more than half drunk." "Well,
well," said Mr. Haynes, "I'm glad there is reformation *begun.*"

   Mr. Haynes was an earnest advocate of a thoroughly educated
ministry; and often expressed his regret that he had not gone
through a regular course of study. A young clergyman conversing
with him on the subject remarked with apparent sincerity, that

he thought ignorant ministers were more likely to succeed than learned ones. "Won't you tell me, then, sir," said Mr. Haynes, "how much ignorance is necessary to make an eminent preacher?"

A neighboring minister, whose house had been burned with all its contents, was stating the circumstance to Mr. Haynes, and expressed special regret that all his manuscript sermons were consumed. "Don't you think, Brother," replied Mr. Haynes, "that they gave more light from the fire than they ever did from the pulpit?"

He once met a minister who had been on a tour through the northern part of the state, preaching false and pernicious sentiments, and said to him, "You have been on a preaching tour, I understand; what success do you have?" "Good success," was the reply, "very good success, great success; the devil himself can never destroy such a cause." "You needn't be concerned about that," replied Mr. Haynes; "he never will try."

Rev. Herman Ball, of East Rutland, persisted in remaining unmarried, very much against the wishes of his people, some of whom requested Mr. Haynes to exert his influence with Mr. Ball to change his manner of life. This he was very willing to do, being, indeed, already in the habit of rallying his friend severely upon his bachelor life. He was put on the defensive sooner than he expected, by Mr. Ball's saying that he had been thinking seriously on the subject, and had about concluded to change his condition, by taking one of brother Haynes's daughters to wife. But the rejoinder was instantaneous: "I greatly respect my Brother Ball; but I also love my daughters, and I cannot think of throwing one of them away by such an arrangement." The thought that a Doctor of Divinity was not a good match for the daughter of a colored man, must have operated on Mr. Ball's nerves like an electric shock.

At a certain election, both the candidates for an important office were open and avowed infidels, and rather notorious for their infidelity; as a consequence of which, a great many persons would not vote at all. On the day of election Mr. Haynes went to a neighboring town to see a friend, who greeted him with the question, "Well, Father Haynes, did you put in your vote for ———, before you left home?" "No," was the prompt reply, "no, when there are two candidates up, and one is Satan and the other the Old Boy, I don't think it is much object to vote."

Danby At the annual meeting, 1783, at the house of Stephen Calkins, *Rutland Co.* Ebenezer Wilson, moderator, it was
Vol. III
    "Voted that if any man in the town of Danby, shall bring the small pox into the town, by way of innoculation, or by carelessness or neglect after having the same, shall be liable to pay a fine of ten pounds, lawful money, to the treasurer of the town."

    That disease was prevailing in some of the towns in the county to an alarming extent.

Brandon Jedidiah Winslow, Sept. 28, 1791, was disciplined "for boiling *Rutland Co.* maple sap upon the Lord's day." Dea. Winslow said he was *Vol. III* "sorry that he did it, on the account of it being a grief to the minds of his breatherin, but not owing himself therin gilty of a breach of the Sabbath," he insisted "that he therein was himself in the way of his duty." But "the Church vuing it a direct violation of the Law of god, and that he might as well be employed in a most any other bisness taking that with the matter of exSample undder ConSideration—they voted not satisfied. Upon which Brother winslow requested a CounSell and the Church redily complied, then proceded and Mutually Chose the west Church in Rutland for the odd Church, then the Choice by vote of the Church in Jericho and the Church in Orwell and Mr. Winslow made Choice of the Church in Hinsdale and the Church in Walpole, To meet the last Thursday in January next."

    Whether the "conSell" ever met, and if so, what disposition they made of the case, the records do not say.

For many years moose were abundant, and contributed much *St. Johnsbury* toward supplying the wants of the settlers. How Daniel Hall, in *Caledonia Co.* 1793, gat for himself the necessaries of life, and the name of a *Vol. I* mighty hunter, may be gathered from the following notes, inserted as they were taken from the narrator:

"Hall had grant of land from Dr. Arnold—hundred acres—in

St. Johnsbury—west of Passumpsic—above Plain—by mistake, deed not given—next year Doctor dies—alarming apprehensions —Hall applies to Josias Lyndon—son of Doctor—J. L. gives him hundred acres—up in Lyndon—Hall satisfied—next morning up early—packs wife and goods on hand sled—travels to Lyndon— on crust—unpacks wife and goods—builds fire—sets up wigwam —moves in wife and goods—all settled sundown—Next morning, nothing to eat—takes gun—sallies into forest—tracks a moose— big one—shoots moose—skins thigh—cuts out steak—carries home —wife delighted—heard gun go off—thought breakfast coming—

roasts meat on forked stick—eats—no butter, pepper, salt—after breakfast calls up all neighbors—they skin moose—each takes a piece—Hall gets out hand sled—loads on moose meat and pelt—goes to St. Johnsbury—trades—gets three pecks potatoes, half bushel meal, peck salt—carries home to wife—wife delighted—sundown."

Essex County Vol. 1 In laying before the reader the incidents of our early history, I think that some extracts from Eben Judd's diary are as good an account of the early settlers as can be given. He surveyed this portion of Vermont, as well as northern New Hampshire, and many incidents in his journal will show his connection with both localities.

"*Sept. 7th, 1786.* Crossed the river at noon to Joseph Wait's, surveyed on the river the Governor's lot in Brunswick."

"*Sept. 9th.* Finished Governor's lot, &C."

"*Sept. 10th.* Went to meeting at Mr. Hall's in Maidstone. In the afternoon went to Mr. Rich's, and saw his son sick with consumption."

"*Sept. 12th.* Began to survey at Lemington upper bounds."

"*Sept. 13th and 14th.* Surveyed at Lemington and on the river against that place."

"*Sept. 15th.* Surveyed against Minnhead; and camped in the woods."

"*Sept. 17th.* Went to Nath'l Wait's in forenoon, and drew a tooth for his wife. In the afternoon went to old Mr. Blodgett's and heard David Judd preach."

"*Sept. 30th.* Run until we came to the line between Lewis and Magog, there we went on side line to the mile tree southerly, which tree stands on a very high mountain, where we could overlook nearly all of Lewis and some part of Wenlock and Averill."

"*Oct. 2d.* Finished the lotting of Lewis and set out homewards. Lodged on a branch of the Nulhegan river."

"*Oct. 5th.* This day had a meeting at Wooster's. Maj. Wilder mad. Joseph Holdbrook confused the whole meeting and conducted in a scandalous manner; was for having Whitelaw's survey or location all broken up, and all our allotments, and said he was ashamed of such conduct. The meeting was adjourned until the next day, and the settlers of Maidstone sent for."

"*Oct. 7th. and 8th.* Surveyed up the valley of the Connecticut."

"*Oct. 9th.* Surveyed on side of the river in Maidstone. Just at sunset met a company of men on a piece of land that Mr. Shoff lived on. They held our chainmen, and said if we went on they would break our heads. We returned to Thomas Wooster's. (We went on with our work until the 13th.)"

"*Oct. 21st.* Run a line about 4 miles on a high mountain, which is 77 rods perpendicular height."

"*Oct. 22d.* Run about 4 miles on the east line of Stratford, over a large pond. Good land all around it, and a fine path made by moose."

"*Oct. 27.* Lodged at John Holdbrook's in Stratford, and eat old hasty pudding that the old man had made a week before." [He leaves his boarding place on account of high charges, being 10 shillings per week for himself, and horse keeping besides.]

"*Nov. 8th.* Surveyed on the river in Maidstone [was stopped and held fast by the settlers of said town near Merrill's] finally they desisted." He then says, "We compromised, and they agreed to delay the matter till after the Surveyor's meeting, by our promising to use our influence to have each settler have 20 acres of meadow and 80 acres of upland. Great indignation was expressed against the doings and usage of Holdbrook."

"*Nov. 30th.* Thanksgiving day in Vermont. Went to Mr. Hall's at night. Fine supper—roasted turkey, chicken pie, and the first apples and apple pie I have tasted since I came to Coos. Had a fiddler and Coos dance. Went from there to Mr. Lucas's about 10 o'clock at night, where we found a company drinking sizzled rum, or hot toddy. Had a high caper, as it is called. About midnight returned to Esq. Eames, and made out to get to bed without help. The weather moderated about this time, as might have been expected."

"*Dec. 3d.* A disease very prevalent among young women, and some boys have it—large bunch on their throats or bronchial. About two-thirds or more of girls and young women have these bronchial bunches which are frequently as large as a hen's egg. Do not generally prove fatal."

"*June 4th, 1787.* Crossed the river to Williston to see his excellency, Governor Chittenden of Vermont. I found him in a small house in the woods"—

Questions and Answers:

"Ques.: In what manner must the surveyor be paid for running the outlines of the towns?

"Ans.: Those towns which were settled and located before the war, the State of Vermont will pay for running the outlines.

"Ques.: (After showing him the advertisement and votes of our meeting) Will this meeting answer our purpose to act upon or not?

"Ans.: You had better warn a new meeting and take regular steps of the law, and then you need not fear about having any thing overhauled.

"Ques.: Will it be likely that we shall get a new grant of land to make up the deficiency in those towns that fall short according to charter?

"Ans.: This state would not wish to make up the damage done by New Hampshire, but if you have paid more money for towns than you ought, the legislature will undoubtedly give you that back in lands. That will ever be my advice. You can draw a petition for that purpose and bring to the assembly, and I will overlook it and see it is well stated, &c. You can as well do it yourself as to employ any one else to do it. It will be best to set forth how much your land falls short from the charter, and then cast up and see how much you have paid over what you ought to have paid, and I will help you all I can. You can, if you like, petition for Lunenburgh, to make up the deficiency, and then pay what the overplus tax money will not pay.

"QUES.: What shall we do with settlers now on pitches in the towns?

"ANS.: You must put into the warning for the meeting to have them hold their pitches, and you must not interrupt them, for I will take the part of the poor settlers rather than have them interrupted. You must give them more than granted, if you intend to have them peaceable."

None of our first settlers were possessed of much property. With perhaps one or two exceptions none had any thing more than enough to pay for the first purchase of their lands, and supply themselves with provisions for a year, and the necessary team and tools to commence a settlement. A few only possessed property to that extent. A majority had to purchase their lands on credit and rely upon their own industry to pay for their lands and support themselves and families. The ax and the firebrand were the only aids which most of the first settlers had in reclaiming the forest and providing for the sustenance of themselves and their families. The difficulties in making purchases, and procuring titles to land embarrassed the operations and impeded the progress of the just settlers. The lands of the valley were owned by nonresidents, and the agents who had the care of the lands generally resided abroad. This led to a species of speculation called "making pitches," which enhanced the price of land and diverted the time and attention of individuals from more regular and industrious pursuits, and it is remarkable that the abuse should have been tolerated at all.

Troy Orleans Co. Vol. III

The mode of operation was this: An individual would, to use the current phrase, "Pitch a lot" that is, he would select a lot and take possession of it by felling a few trees, and then apply to the distant agent for the lot. Even the ceremony of making any sort of communication with the agent was not always observed. By thus making his "Pitch" the individual, by a sort of common law of the valley, or usage which was recognized among the settlers, acquired a pre-emption right to the lot, so that no person who really desired to purchase and settle on it could do so without first buying the "pitcher's" or squatter's claim. By this ridiculous species of speculation a kind of monopoly was created, the best lots were occupied and prices were enhanced.

One of the oldest settlers, Dea. Hovey, asserts, that when he came into the valley, in 1803, he found all the best lots, those he wished to purchase were "pitched," or covered by these sham claims. To encourage settlers, Mr. Hauxhurst had previously reduced the price of five lots in his gore to 50 cents per acre, these were "pitched" of course and Dea. Hovey says that he selected and purchased one of these lots for which he paid $200, of which sum $50 only were paid to Mr. Hauxhurst's agent and $150 were pocketed by the speculator or man who made the pitch.

Coventry
Orleans Co.
Vol. III
At the time of the chartering of Coventry, and for many years after, Orleans County was destitute of inhabitants, and inaccessible by roads, and lands were of no value except for speculative purposes. Buel purchased the rights of his associates, one by one, as he had opportunity, paying from £5 to £20, and in a few instances as much as £30, for each right; until in 1788, the title of 54 of the 60 rights was vested in him. His deeds, however, were not put on record until 1801, and, in the meantime, sales for taxes, and levies of executions against the original proprietors had created conflicting titles to much of the land. In 1791 all the lands in town were sold to Stephen Pearl, Sheriff of Chittenden County, to satisfy a land tax of a half-penny an acre levied by the Legislature of Vermont. Ira Allen purchased most of them, and 49 rights, which were not redeemed within the prescribed time, were

deeded to him. Buel afterwards quitclaimed to Allen his interest in those rights, and appears to have had little or no more to do with the township.

Allen made few, if any sales of his Coventry lands till 1798. In March of that year he was in London, where he met Stephen Bayard, of Philadelphia, and sold him the 2,000 acres comprised in Coventry Gore for the round sum of £1,600 sterling, ($7,104). There is something ludicrous in the minute particularity of English forms of conveyancing as exhibited in the deed 6 pages long, by which Allen transferred these 2,000 acres of woods and mountains, "together with all and singular houses, outhouses, edifices, buildings, paths, passages, commons, fishing places, hedges, ditches, gates, stiles, fences, ways, waters, water-courses, lights, liberties, casements, privileges, profits, commodities, advantages, hereditaments, and appurtenances whatsoever." If Bayard paid the purchase money, or any part of it, it was a dead loss to him, for in the following July a direct land-tax was assessed by the Congress of the United States, to satisfy which, the whole town of Coventry, including the Gore, was sold at auction at the house of Thomas Tolman, in Greensboro, May 20, 1801, by James Paddock of Craftsbury, the collector, for $4.80, and was never redeemed. Jabez G. Fitch of Vergennes, was the purchaser. William C. Harrington, of Burlington, had a color of title to 8 rights; Reed Ferris, of Pawlington, N. Y., to 9; Alexander Schist, of Canada, to 15; Thaddeus Tuttle, of Burlington, to 15; and James Seaman, of the City of New York, to 16. Fitch bought the interests of them all, and Dec. 14, 1801, he took a conveyance of Ira Allen's entire title. By these means he became the ostensible owner of the whole township, and had a valid title to nearly all of it.

It was by Fitch's agency that the settlement of the town was effected. He offered land at moderate prices to actual settlers, promising gifts of land to some, (which promises, however, were fulfilled in few, if any, instances,) and encouraged emigration as much as possible. Two dollars an acre was the current price of land, with a liberal credit, and cash was seldom required. Most of the early purchasers made their payments in "good clean wheat" or "merchantable neat cattle, (bulls and stags excepted,) not exceeding eight years old." In many of the conveyances he reserved to himself "two thirds of the iron ore being and growing on the land," a reservation which never proved of any value. Notwithstanding the pains he took to purchase all outstanding claims, the titles to some of the lands afterwards proved defective, and subjected his grantees to serious loss.

Orange Co. Rev. Elijah Lyman used to be called far and near to attend
Vol. II Councils, especially in cases of litigation. He used to succeed wonderfully in getting the parties to settle without a verdict.

One time in Rochester he got the parties to settle and weep and pray together before he went home. On parting with them he told them, "We have got the fire most out; but you may find some sparks now and then; and if you do, run for a bucket of water and quench it as soon as possible."

Grafton In 1785, March 21, they voted at the town meeting that all their
Windham Co. ox sleds should be four feet wide. In this warrant was an article
Vol. V to see if the town would take any steps towards building a meeting house, but no action was taken.

Bradford Disturbers of the peace were liable to be set in the stocks, a sort
Orange Co. of frame to confine the feet between two pieces of timber; and
Vol. II thieves, counterfeiters, and such-like characters, to be tied up to a whipping-post, and receive a certain number of lashes, laid on the bare shoulders, with a cat-o'-nine tails; an instrument of punishment, says Webster, "consisting of nine pieces of line or

cord, fastened to a piece of thick rope, and having each three knots at intervals; used to flog offenders on board of ships." In some instances criminals were branded with some ignominious mark on the cheek, as with an R for rogue, or L for liar; or had the rim of an ear cut away.

Even in this town, were a set of stocks, and a whipping-post. They stood on the east side of Main Street, near where you turn to go down to the paper-mill. These punishments were more generally inflicted at Chelsea, near the jail, but even here, Sheriff Barron occasionally exercised his authority, by laying the lashes on the back of some luckless culprit tied to the whipping-post. The names of two or three of these transgressors have been given me; but why should they be perpetuated with dishonor; it is a matter of rejoicing that such barbarous corporal punishments are no longer in use among us.

It was voted to hold future town meetings at the house of Abraham Chase, and that a sign post and stocks should be set up near the house of Abraham Chase. It was also voted to build a town pound upon the east side of the town. The erection of a sign post and stocks, referred to above, was agreable to a law of the State, passed in 1779, which act was *Dunby Rutland Co. Vol. III*

"That every town in this State shall make and maintain at their own charge, a good pair of stocks, with a lock and key sufficient to hold and secure such offenders as shall be sentenced to sit therein; which stock shall be set in the most public place in each respective town; and in the same place there shall be a sign post erected and set up, at the charge of the town, and maintained in sufficient repairs; on which sign post all notifications, warrants, &C., for meetings shall be set up."

According to the laws of that time, criminal offences were punishable by whipping on the naked back, from 10 to 100 lashes, according to the nature of the offense.

Fairfax
Franklin Co.
Vol. II The first school taught in North Fairfax was by David Sears. These early schools were generally taught in private houses in the winter, and in summer, some barn was occupied for a school-house. I asked the oldest resident of the town, Beriah Beeman, to describe to me the old school-houses of the first settlers:

"They," said he, "were built of logs, with a huge fire-place in one end, and a door in the other, on each side was one window. The desks were made by driving pegs into side-logs, and upon these placing unplaned boards. The seats were made movable."

This was a great improvement upon private rooms. In these houses did the first generation of the town receive their education. Here they conned their spelling-books, and testaments, and practiced at their copy-books—becoming good readers, correct spellers and fair penmen. If by chance, an arithmetic or a geography was obtained, the owners were prepared to become the leaders of the school, and were looked up to as prodigies in their circles. In asking old teachers the wages received, their reply was but little more than board. The story still holds current, that one of these early candidates for schoolmaster's honors, on making application for a school, was asked his terms, and that he, looking at the wide mouthed fireplace, answered that he thought he could cut the wood and teach the school for the ashes he could make.

THE STATE SEAL

Bennington
Bennington Co.
Vol. I Henry Stevens, Esq., the State Antiquarian, gives the following account of the origin of the seal of Vermont.

"I had heard that the Vermont coat of arms originated in Arlington, and stopped there to obtain reliable authority for the story, some years, since as I was returning from a visit to Bennington. I had in my pocket the guard-roll of Governor Chit-

tenden; an old man was pointed out to me as one of this Company. I joined him, introduced myself, and walked down with him to his house. It was summer, a warm day, about noon, and we sat down in the porch before the door, where some vines grew and it was cool to have a chat. I asked him if he was one of Chittenden's guard. He was proud as a peacock to be asked. I showed him the roll, there was his name, and he informed me that he was the only man of the Company then living. I asked where he boarded at the time, "at the Governor's" he replied, "I was a young man and so boarded with him. We had plenty to eat and drink, a good place it was." Said I do you remember any thing of the drinking cups? "Yes, they were of horn." Had any of them any mark or marks on them? "Yes, the seal of our State was first engraved on one of them, I have drank out of it many a time.

An English lieutenant, who used to secretly bring letters to the Governor, was there one time, "sparking" the Governor's hired girl; he stopped several days, and taking a view from the west window of the Governor's residence of a wheat field, some two acres in the distance, beyond which was a knoll with one solitary pine upon its top, he engraved it upon this cup. The field was fenced off from a level space intervening between the house, within this space he put "the cow" with her head over the fence for the grain. The Governor's drinking cups were made from the horn of an ox, and bottomed with wood. First was cut off a cup from the lower end of the horn that measured half a pint, next a gill cup, then a third cup which was a "glass."

The engraved cup attracted the notice of Ira Allen, who adopted its device for our State Seal; only when he took hold of it he brought the cow over the fence into the midst of the grain— bundles on either side, so when she had eaten one stack the other was ready."

3

The Federal Period, 1791 to 1825

Permanent capital established at Montpelier in 1805 : University of Vermont opened in 1800 : Embargo Act before War of 1812 stimulated growth of manufacturing : Wholesale smuggling of provisions to British forces garrisoned in Canada during the war : Battle of Plattsburgh gave Americans effective control of Lake Champlain by 1814 : Famine year of "1816 and froze to death" increased emigration from Vermont to the West.

"THE STATE OF VERMONT is a vast country, situated east of New Hampshire, south of Massachusetts, and west of New York. It is one hundred and fifty-five miles in length, and sixty in breadth. The capital of the State is Bennington.

Bennington Bennington Co. Vol. 1

"The Allens are the chiefs, or head men, of the country. It is governed by its own laws, independent of Congress and the States. Hitherto, it has been an object of contention between the States of New York and New Hampshire. The people had for a long time no other name than Green Mountain Boys, which they

Gallicized into Verdmont, and afterwards corrupted into the easier pronunciation of Vermont." From an 1808 English Geography

Lowell
Orleans Co.
Vol. III In the early history of the town, when there were but four or five residents, the male portion met at the house of Maj. Walker, "according to the custom of their fathers," to celebrate the anniversary of the Independence of the United States. They were destitute of any piece of ordnance, yet feeling that their celebration would not accord with the custom of their fathers, they were led to invent one. It was made by boring a hole in a hard-wood stump and then filling it with powder and inserting a plug. The day was thus spent in firing their *cannon*, which reverberated from the surrounding hills, kindling within them, with the aid of the "ruby wine," an unusual degree of patriotism. After the celebration was over, Maj. Walker remarked, "*Well, we have had a poorty good celebration.*"

The company separated, agreeing to meet at Mr. White's the next Thanksgiving. Accordingly, Mr. John Harding and wife, Maj. Walker and wife, James Caldwell and his sister Charlotte and Miss Sarah Brigham, repaired to Mr. White's. All except two (who rode horseback), were gathered into a lumber-sleigh, drawn by a pair of oxen. The river being very high, the sleigh had to answer for a boat in passing over the hollows on the mead. To make the company full, Abel Curtis followed on foot, arriving there just before dusk.

The house was small—not more than 16 or 18 feet square. It was built of rough logs with a large fire-place at one end. The company was well served with a supper. My informant does not distinctly remember what it consisted, excepting that the mince pies were highly seasoned with pepper, which gave to the mouth a peculiar sensation, which was only relieved by drawing large draughts of air. Supper being over, the company enjoyed themselves as best they could, until a late hour. They all slept in the same room excepting a few who were stowed away in the small space overhead. After breakfast the next morning they all dispersed to their homes.

Alexander Kathan (1729–1825) kept a memorandum in almanacs *Dummerston* for each year, of principal events in his farming business and other *Windham Co.* matters worthy of note. These almanacs were kept in file by *Vol. V* stringing them on a leathern thong.

The earliest of these almanacs is for the year 1764, and the numbers are complete down to the year 1817, except 1795 and 1814. Here are a few items:

"March 19, 1764, tapped trees, made 21 lbs. of molasses."

"February 1765, tapped trees, and sugared off 18 pounds on the 26th."

"April 6, 1778, made off 10 lbs. of sugar; that's the first this season."

"May 19th, 1780, remarkable dark day."

"April 5th, 1781, a man and a horse crossed the river on the ice."

"The 2d Sabbath in the same month snow was knee deep in the field and solid."

"1785, snow 1st day of April, 34 inches deep on a level."

"19th, old snow knee deep, new snow."

"May 26th, put in seine and catch no shad."

"May 30, catch shad."

"March 31st, 1786, no snow."

"2d day of April, terrible storm of wind, and snow fell knee deep."

"17th, began to plow."

"March 29th, 1787, burnt out the bass-wood stub and scart out two flying squirrels."

"May 10th, 1788, the mountains covered with snow."

"Aug. 19th, a hurricane."

"March 1803, what a sight of pigeons did fly all the 13th."

"June 6th, 1804, set tobacco."

"Aug. 29th, cut up tobacco."

"Mrs. Kathan sea a robin on the 9th of February; robins here seen til the 17th."

"March 5th, sea two robins."

"July 12th, had string beans."

"The 22d, had new tatos."

"February 1811, killed 110 rats in the corn house in one day."

Roxbury Some 60 years ago, Moses Claflin, a simple man who lived in this
Washington Co. town, who occasionally made his home with Mr. R., one evening
Vol. IV sat by the fire in a "brown study," and Esq. Roberston sat opposite quietly chewing, and now and then spitting into the broad fireplace. At last Moses looked up and asked, "Squire, what did you learn to chew tobaker for?" Mr. Roberston replied, "Oh, so's to be a gentleman." Moses studied the matter a moment and with great gravity replied, "W'al, ye didn't make out, did ye?"

UP-HILL AND DOWN-HILL POLITICS.

Bennington Nearly all of the Down-hill people, among whom were the
Bennington Co. Deweys, the Swifts and Tichenors, were Federalists, while those
Vol. V of Upper-hill, comprising the Robinsons, the Fays, Haswells and others, were anti-Federalists and friends of Mr. Jefferson, who was soon to become President. They took upon themselves the name of Republicans, disclaiming that of Democrats, which from the excesses that had recently been committed under it during the French Revolution, was unpopular, not to say odious.

The Federalists however dubbed the Republicans with the name of Democrats by way of reproach, and the Republicans retorted by calling them aristocrats and monarchists.

Mr. Tichenor, a native of New Jersey, whose courtly manners and fascinating conversation had acquired for him the familiar title of the "Jersey sleek," and whose great personal popularity had enabled him to obtain ten successive elections of governor, up to the year 1808, while the other State officers were generally chosen by the Republicans, and also a majority of the legislature, was the acknowledged leader of the Federalists; while Jonathan Robinson, who was chief judge of the supreme court from 1801 to 1808, and was then chosen a senator in Congress to fill a vacancy and held the office by another election till 1815, occupied a like leadership of the Republicans. He and Governor Tichenor were both able men and shrewd politicians, and each of them exercised an important, and frequently, a controlling influence over their respective parties through-out the State.

From 1808 to 1813, the Republicans were generally in a majority in the town, and were able to choose members of that party to the assembly, though the elections were often very spirited and close. But during the war with England when the times were hard and taxes high, the Federal candidates were chosen, and at the election in 1813 and 1814, the Federal governor and other state officers were also elected. The Legislature of 1814, also chose Governor Tichenor United States Senator to succeed Judge Robinson.

On the return of peace with England, the Federalists, from the alleged unpatriotic conduct of their prominent leaders during the war, became very unpopular. The Federalists, in fact, ceased to exist as a national party after 1816.

We and a lot of other boys were standing in the street somewhere against our present Court House, when, sudden as the bursting of a thunder clap, the whole village shook with the explosion of the cannon on the State House common. We all instantly ran at the top of our speed for the spot. When we had got about half

Montpelier Washington Co. Vol. IV

way there, we met a gang of other boys from one of the back towns, who taken by surprise and seized with panic at the stunning shock, were fleeing for their lives in the opposite direction; but gaining a little assurance from seeing us rushing toward the scene of their fright, one, braver than the rest, stopped short, boldly faced about and exclaimed, "Hoo! I an't a n'attom afraid!" and all now joining in the race, we were, in another minute, within a few rods of the smoking gun, which had been discharged on the announcement of the election of Isaac Tichenor as Governor. The next moment our attention was attracted by the voice of Israel P. Dana, sheriff of the county, standing on the upper terrace of the State House, and loudly proclaiming, "Hear ye! hear ye! hear ye! The Honorable Paul Brigham has been elected Lieutenant Governor, in and over the State of Vermont, by the suffrages of the freemen. God save the people!"

Bennington
Bennington Co.
Vol. 1

Tichenor's peculiar talent in commending himself to the favor of others, is alleged to have been sometimes used with considerable effect for electioneering purposes. He is said to have had remarkable tact in discovering and lauding the extraordinary good qualities of the farms, horses, cattle and other property and even of the not very promising children of those whose support he desired to obtain. Many anecdotes in relation to this matter were formerly told of him, one of which may serve as a characteristic specimen. While traveling in a distant part of the State, he contrived to pass the residence of a farmer of great influence in his town, who had formerly supported him for governor, but who was now supposed to be wavering. On his approach to the place, he discovered the farmer at some distance building a stone wall by the road-side. Leaving his carriage, the governor began to examine the wall with great care and earnestness, looking over and along both sides of it and exhibiting signs of excessive admiration. On coming within speaking distance, the governor exclaimed with much apparent emotion, "Bless me, friend, what a beautiful and noble wall you are building. I don't believe there is another equal to it in the State." "Yes, Governor," was the reply of the farmer, "it's a very good wall to be sure, but I can't vote for you this year."

It is perhaps to the credit of Glover that its citizens have never been disposed to very great extent, to engage in lawsuits against another, hence, although they have regarded lawyers with respect according to their merits as a class, yet they have never given them any great encouragement.

Glover
Orleans Co.
Vol. III

Before the state prison was built, this town like many others, had its whipping post and stocks. They stood at Charlotte Corner in front of the present residence of Dr. John Strong. A transient person on one occasion stole a cow from Capt. James Hill, for which he was tried before Daniel W. Griswold, Esq, and sentenced to receive ten lashes and pay the costs. The whipping was inflicted by Constable Clark. All remitted their fees to the poor culprit except Griswold, who required him to cut wood for his. Griswold allowed him to lodge on his kitchen floor at night. The next morning it appeared that the incorrigible rascal had decamped during the night, taking with him a new pair of boots which belonged to Griswold.

Charlotte
Chittenden Co.
Vol. I

On training-day mornings, the companies were accustomed to wake up their officers by firing a salute at their doors, for which compliment, his grace, from corporal up to captain, was expected to liberally treat. If any one became intoxicated it was quite disgraceful, but *honorable* to bear up with the largest quantity without intoxication.

Monkton
Addison Co.
Vol. I

The following poetical specimen is from the pen of one of those primitive and untaught bards, Mr. Ebenezer Finney.

MONKTON CANNON.

When men rejoiced in days of yore
That stamp-acts should appear no more,
They fired their pump instead of cannon,
And shook the very earth we stand on.
But latter years, more full of glory,
Since Whig has fairly conquered Tory,
Pump guns are thrown by in disgrace,
And iron stationed in their place.
The heroes of a certain town,
To please themselves and gain renown,
A cannon made, without a blunder,
To send forth home-made peals of thunder.
This thing was formed, our heroes say,
To usher in our training-day;
But ere their training had arrived,
To try her metal they contrived.
In order firm the heroes stand,
'Til the commandant gives command
To load and fire, when at the sound
Hills, dales, and vales—all echo round.
What transport fills these sons of Mars;
They shout for joy, and bless their stars;
But oh, how transient is their fun!
They load too deep, and split their gun.
Earth, at the blast, turns shaking Quaker;
Boys curse the cannon and its maker;
What havoc made 'mongst ducks and hens;
The pigs run frightened round their pens;
Young puppies set up hideous yells,
While goslins perished in their shells;

Lake Champlain shakes from shore to shore,
And Camel's Hump was seen no more.

Henry Willard was a man of property and bought and sold other *Dummerston* farms in town. He kept a large stock of cattle, raised considerable *Windham Co.* grain, but was careful to keep his granaries locked. A friend once *Vol. V* inquired of him why he kept his grain under lock and key. "Your neighbors," said he, "are all honest." "I know it," replied Mr. Willard, "but I want to keep them so."

The early settlers were not noted for their piety or religious at- *Shelburne* tainments. Their habits and customs were not of a religious char- *Chittenden Co.* acter. They were in the habit of using spirituous liquors rather *Vol. I* freely, as was the custom in all other places in those days. They must be had in preference to anything else; were necessary on all occasions and under all circumstances, and were an antidote for all the ills of life and a remedy for every disease. From 1805 to 1815, there was probably more liquor used in Shelburne, and throughout the state, than at any other period of the same number of years before or since. Previous to that time the population was not so great and the facilities for obtaining it were not so good; and from about 1815 there began to be some temperance advocates, and they have been increasing in numbers and influence from that day.

In those days there were some 200 distilleries in the state of Vermont. There were 30 of them in the county of Chittenden, and four of them in the town of Shelburne; and they were all in full operation. There were perhaps from 20 to 25 hogsheads of liquor sold annually at the stores in Shelburne. There was one tavern at the village and four others on the road to Burlington, which made five rum-selling and dram-drinking establishments in so many miles. I have known even ministers of the Gospel who made no secret of taking a glass of grog before entering the pulpit to preach, declaring that it assisted them to preach; and many of their hearers carried their flasks of cider brandy in their pockets to church, and they were freely and fearlessly passed around at intermission, with the understanding that if it assisted the minister to preach, it also assisted them to hear and understand.

Cabot
Washington Co.
Vol. IV
Twelve distilleries were in full blast at one time in Cabot. These made whiskey very plenty, and it was used in all the different callings of life. Some even thought it was cheaper than corn for common living. It is said one poor man in Plainfield used to say that he would buy a half bushel of corn-meal, and carry it home, and his wife would make it all up into hasty pudding, and the children would eat it all up and go to bed crying with hunger. But let him buy a gallon of whisky, and they would all go to sleep like kittens by the fire; he thought whisky the cheapest diet.

On all public days whisky went around freely, and officers all had to treat. March meeting, 1806, tradition says the whiskey was kept in the closet of the school-house where the meeting was held, which was imbibed so frequently by candidates and their supporters, some of them got so they hardly knew which way to vote. About middle way of the proceedings of the meeting it was "voted that the door leading into the closet be shut and kept so for the space of one-half hour."

St. Albans
Franklin Co.
Vol. II
The first Tuesday in June was the day fixed by the laws of the State, for the annual inspection and drill. Its coming has been anxiously awaited. With the earliest streak of dawn, squads of the younger and more ardent soldiery assembled in front of the dwellings of their principal officers, to fire a morning salute. The report

Montpelier

of the heavily loaded guns rung out upon the still, clear air of morning, roaring down the valleys, and awakening a thousand echoes along the hill-sides, rousing whole neighborhoods prematurely, to the glories and the fatigues of the day. The officer thus honored appeared in his door-way in dishabille, and invited his comrades in arms to enter and partake of refreshments which had been provided over right, in anticipation of the visit.

The staple refreshment was whisky, and under its influence, a continued popping of firearms was kept up, until some time after sunrise. But at length, there is a movement toward the village where the training is to be holden. People of all ages, many with arms and more without, in wagons, on horseback and on foot, are passing along the highways and coming in across-lots. The village is soon alive with men and boys. The taverns, stores and shops are full. The barkeepers in their shirt-sleeves are doing a lively business, and the music of the toddy-stick is incessant.

Among the drinks of the old time was blackstrap, a compound of rum and molasses, which was quite too popular with the young men and boys, many of whom were by its use, started upon a career of intemperance and ruin. Flags flutter, drums rattle, and arms glisten in the sun-beams. In the parlor of the hotel sit the commissioned officers, stiff and stately in their unaccustomed toggery. In a corner near by stands a table, spread with the inevitable decanters, at which the guests are invited to help themselves. The white-haired old soldiers of the Revolution come round, and are among those who require no second invitation. At length the long roll sounds from the drums, the orderly serjeant comes upon the scene armed with a spontoon, and calls on every man to fall in. The squad marches up and down the street, rapidly augmenting in numbers, and is finally paraded upon the green. Capt. Taplin, of Montpelier, was less successful. His company was deficient in that *esprit de corps*, which is so essential to all improvement. The men considered military duty a thing to be gotten rid of when it could be and when it could not, then to be endured and got along with in the easiest manner possible.

On a certain June training-day, they were marching about the streets of Montpelier. The captain, tall, erect and bony, enthusiastic, and filled with martial fire to his very fingers' ends, was marshaling his command with an energy which won the admiration of all beholders. A fine brass-band which he had hired for the occasion, filled the air with spirit-stirring music, and Capt. Taplin was the proudest and the happiest of men. As they went "marching along," he turned into a different street without giving an order to wheel. Going on with head erect and military stride, he all at once wheeled suddenly about, to execute some brilliantly conceived movement for the gratification of the crowd, when to his utter consternation, he saw his company, plodding complacently along the street he had just abandoned, leaving him with the band, alone in his glory.

General trainings were often closed by a mock battle, or (as it was called) a shamfight. They never became very popular. In one of these bloodless contests, an ambush had been laid for a party approaching. The men in ambush, seemed to be opposed to the taking of any unchivalrous advantage over their opponents. There they lay, concealed to be sure, but with fifes and drums playing their loudest strains.

Westminster Windham Co. Vol. V A hotel existed in the parish before there was a meeting-house, or a schoolhouse. The first was kept by Joseph Ide, near the top of the hill, on the old road that leads from E. R. Goodell's to Geo. A. Goodell's. It was a log-house and did a large business in toddy. This was a necessity to meet the wants of the traveling community as early as 1790.

A remnant of the account book, for 1815, shows that the good people of the parish were none too temperate. The following is a specimen of account, leaving out the name:

"*Dr.* to 1 glass of toddy, to 2 toddy, to 3 toddys, to 2 milk-pans, to 10 lbs. hog's lard." This history is this: The debtor got drunk, and mistook his door, and fell down in the pantry, and pulled down after him two pans of milk and a pan of lard, yet warm from the kettle. He was now ready to make his mark in the world. It was training day and he was too noisy and a little too drunk to be respectable.

The captain, a neighbor of his, undertook to get him out of the way. Having exhausted his patience in flattery, and ignorant of the affairs in the pantry, he came to a close hug with the tipsy man, and by a hard struggle shut him up in the barn, when, Lo and behold, he found his buff pants and vest unfit for a captain to wear.

A certain street, west of the center village, has four years been known as "Poverty Lane"; and the origin is this: *Brookfield Orange Co. Vol. II*

Of the two Lyman brothers, the one who lived on the west street was a temperance man, while the other was a lover of tippling. As the former was on one occasion inviting his neighbors and townsmen to a "raising," he was jocosely told by his brother that if he would furnish liquor for his men his street should receive a good name, but if he was so niggardly as to refuse, it should be christened "Poverty Lane." As he adhered strictly to his temperance principles, the name was coupled with the street in good earnest; though like many of our common names it is, and has always been, as great a misnomer as that of the "man in the moon."

After post offices began to be established, and letters carried in the mail, the postage of a single letter, any distance less than 300 miles was 10 cents—over that distance 25 cents; and if it consisted of two pieces, ever so small, double those rates. *Hubbardton Rutland Co. Vol. III*

An aged lady was subjected to the necessity of paying 50 cents for a single half sheet, with a little scrap of calico, just to show the figure of a new dress her daughter-in-law had lately bought, and the main letter was on the subject of the dress. Her 50-cent piece would almost balance the whole. She felt herself injured, and would never have taken the letter from the office, if she could have got at its contents without sparing her hard earned half dollar. And so with hundreds of others; and many had to lie in the office—were refused and treated as dead letters.

Whitingham The liberality of the town in allowing its citizens to pay their
Windham Co. taxes in "truck and dicker," and the raising of money by games
Vol. V of chance did not turn out to be a complete remedy for all the financial ills, and numerous farms were sold under the hammer.

Brookfield During the visit of the Prince of Wales to this country, not many
Orange Co. years after the close of the Revolution, that bigoted scion of roy-
Vol. II ·alty passed through Vermont, on his way to Canada. In the northern part of Brookfield resided Abner Pride, a shoemaker by trade, and, as his house was a long way from any other, it was frequently made a stopping-place by travelers. The Prince called here for refreshment, on his journey, and, when about to take his leave, stepped up to Mrs. Pride, with saucy freedom, and kissed her. Observing that she showed signs of resentment, he remarked, soothingly, "Oh, never mind; you can now tell your people that you have had the honor of being kissed by an English Prince." Mr. Pride, from his work at his bench, had witnessed the scene and, hearing these words, rose indignantly, and, with a kick, more forcible than graceful, ejected the impertinent prince from the door, sending after him this mocking farewell, "O, never mind; you can now go home and tell your people that you have had the honor of being kicked out of doors by an American cobbler."

[I have the following account in his own words, which I took down from his lips, as he narrated it to me some years since.– A.M.H., Ed.]

"September 14, 1814—The day of the election at St. Albans, after the election, Sanford Gadcomb, Solomon Walbridge, son of the old sheriff of St. Albans, and myself, started to go to Plattsburgh, as soldiers, on horseback, through Georgia and Milton. At the sand-bar there [at Milton] we attempted to cross over, having stopped a few moments at Fox's tavern, this side of the lake. It was a mile across the bar, dark—or only star-light, and I told Gadcomb it looked too much like going to sea horseback in the night, and I did not like to cross. The wind blew strong from the north, but Gadcomb thought he could cross without difficulty, though the swells ran so high and dashed so upon the shore.

St. Albans Franklin Co. Vol. II

"We urged our horses in with difficulty, but we proceeded till we saw a light upon the opposite shore, which we supposed had been lighted to pilot us across, and we advanced till about half way over, when the water began to deepen, the swells from the north rolling hard against us, till our horses drifting off the north side of the bar, were afloat. Gadcomb was forward, I in the middle, Walbridge behind, each about 3 rods distant. Gadcomb undertook to swim his horse forward to shore, Walbridge behind, said his horse wanted to turn round and go back. My horse stood right up and down—in no swimming condition. In about two minutes Walbridge cried out, 'My horse touches bottom,' and my horse at once righted in a swimming condition and pursued his horse.

"Meantime I had climbed upon the saddle from which I slid when my horse lost bottom, and we were soon back on the bar again where the water was not more than knee-deep to our horses. Gadcomb was out of sight and I cried out, 'We are on good ground,' but he understood us to cry we were in trouble. Walbridge and I came out on shore where we entered, when we repeatedly hallooed, and receiving no answer from any quarter, supposed Gadcomb was drowned and started to go back to Fox's tavern, but on our way through the swamp, moving along slowly near the shore, we heard somebody halloo, and answered. The halloo was kept up back and forth till we found it was Gadcomb, who had swam ashore, we all returned to the tavern wet as water could make us, and remained about two hours, till the moon was up, and about a hundred had collected to cross; so that when we crossed, which at length was nicely done, the line of them reached clear across the bar.

"After we got over the bar, we went up to the old landlord's who kept tavern on South Island, where we stayed the remainder of the night. While here, the landlord stated that he hoped we should get whipped by the British, and that all would get off from the bar who attempted to cross. This raised my ideas, and I told him we should hear no such talk on our route, that we were going to Plattsburgh to fight for our country, and we could fight before we got there, if necessary, and the effect was sufficient to stop that Tory's noise.

"We went down the next morning and waited for a sloop to take us across. About 2 o'clock, P.M., the sloop arrived and took us over to Plattsburgh. This was Wednesday. We remained there 'in battle' till Sunday night. Sunday, the last day of the battle, the British forded the river against what is called Pike's old encampment, with their whole force, 13,000 strong. They forded the river, and advanced into the pine plains, where the Vermont and New York volunteers were distant about 80 or 100 rods. The woods were full of Vermont and New York volunteers, every man fighting for himself, all on the Irishman's own hook, and we were so hard upon them that they were compelled to retreat, and we pursued them like a band of blood-hounds back to the river, their dead and wounded scattered along the way.

"In crossing the river they lost many guns and some of the men floated down stream,—retreating up the river, the enemy were soon, however, out of our sight. That night they retreated back to Canada, leaving a good many deserters in the village of Platts- burgh. On their camp-ground their supplies were many of them left. On Sunday, the winding up battle-day, about 200 of us went down from Pike's encampment toward our fort, and when we could see a picket guard on the other side of the river, we would fire at him, and when we could not see a redcoat to fire at, still we would all fire, so as to have the enemy understand the woods were all full of soldiers for two miles in length along the shore, and when we got opposite Plattsburgh village and attempted to cross the bridge, the British poured in a volley upon us. Only one was wounded, the bullets passing directly over our heads, one bullet passing within 12 inches of me, cutting off a little twig so I could see where the little fellow had tripped along. We returned up the river the same way as we came down."

During the war of 1812, the inhabitants of this town became much alarmed on account of the Indians. The inhabitants of all the ad- jacent towns, northerly, were so fearful of an attack, that they left their homes at night, and several families were grouped to- gether for safety, meeting at one house after another, in the vari- ous neighborhoods, while the panic continued. *Brownington Orleans Co. Vol. III*

Some people who left town at that time, never returned, and in consequence lost much of their property, and many who re- mained lost a great deal by attempting to smuggle goods into Canada, or from thence into the States; while a few, more success- ful in their attempts, acquired a large amount of wealth. It is to be regretted that there were any who had so little love for their country as to smuggle cattle over the line, to sell to the British; but such was the case. The plan of procedure was to buy as many cattle as they could, and drive them round through the woods so as to elude the custom-house officers, and, if successful, they were able to sell to the British at very great prices; thus feeding the enemy, while they enriched themselves.

[We think the writer should say, "thus enriching themselves through feeding the enemy." It was not the enemy at all, but their pockets, that it came first in their purpose to serve.—A.M.H., Ed.]

Pawlet   A description of the school-house and school in which we re-
Rutland Co. ceived our education from 1811 to 1820: A plain plank building,
Vol. III   on one end an immense stone-chimney, through which there was a grand prospect of the sky, and whose jaws would hold a half-cord of wood—a writing table running round next the wall; a row of benches in front made of slabs inverted, supported on pins like carpenter's horses; a few low benches in the center; a desk in the corner next to the chimney on which lay the ferule.

The teacher would call the school to order and invest one of the scholars with the rule whose duty it was to pass the rule to the first transgressor of the rules of school, who relieved guard, and passed it to the next delinquent, and so on, with the comforting assurance whoever got the rule twice, or had it when school closed should have it applied to his own palm. The plan served its purpose; order and stillness prevailed. These ferulings were no joke.

We have seen ridges raised on both the hands of a delicate girl who would laugh in the face of the master while a cowardly boy would make a loud outcry and be let off easily. It was a matter of principle with the children not to cry if they could help doing so.

When flagellations failed, we were sometimes required to extend our arm at a right angle with a heavy rule or book in our hand, the master standing near to rap our knuckles if our arm fell below a horizontal line. Or we would be seated on an andiron or a block of wood near the chimney-corner, which would be called a dunce-block and the scholars be required to point the finger of scorn at us, and when wholly incorrigible, as a last resort we would be placed between two girls. We wilted then. But alas! Such was the hardening nature of this capital punishment, its frequent repetition reconciled us to it, and as we grew older, we even began to relish it.

Arithmetic was taught the boys, and needlework the girls (in Summer), all learned reading, writing and spelling. Proficiency in spelling was the test of scholarship. Webster's old spelling book was at our tongues end and the English Reader learned by heart. The teacher would set our copies and mend our goose-quill pens and pay little further attention to our writing. The solution of the problems in Adam's old arithmetic was the work of years. Grammar was studied by the large boys in winter.

Mr. Ralph Rice, was one of the first merchants in town, and was largely engaged in making potash, which he marketed in Montreal. It is said that at one time he took $1300 in gold for that commodity. He sold "calico" from 25 to 50 cents per yard; Bohea tea at $1.25; India cotton, a sleazy, stiff, coarse cloth, from 60 to 75 per yard, and other articles in proportion. Afterwards Walter Tyler kept store in a building a little south of Col. Page's. His stock in trade was quite small. When a customer once proposed to buy a couple dozen buttons, his reply was, "I don't wholesale." *Essex Chittenden Co. Vol. I*

There were some who were not prospered in their worldly possessions, and from year to year there were quite lively times in warning such persons out of town to prevent their becoming a town charge. *Cabot Washington Co. Vol. IV*

[If a family came to want that had been duly "warned out," the town was not obliged to assist them; but if not, the town was liable. A very uncharitable record to put down for all our early towns; if we could not add, it was usually about as serious a matter as appointing a hog ward, to which office every man in town married during the year, even the minister, was a candidate for at next March meeting. The old settlers were fond of practical jokes, and received them very complacently. I have seen the record

where the warning out went so far every family in town was
warned out.—A.M.H., Ed.]

THE GREAT WOLF HUNT ON IRISH HILL IN THE WINTER OF 1803.

Berlin
Washington Co.
Vol. IV

Up to that time it was not known with any certainty that there
were wolves in this section of the county. Several settlers in the
vicinity of the extensive mountain forest called Irish Hill, had lost
sheep; whether they were killed by bears, catamounts, or wolves
was a matter of conjecture; but the (a) boy's perilous adventure
which spread rapidly among the nearest settlements and was im-
plicitly believed at once, established the fact in the minds of all
that there was really a gang of wolves in the vicinity, and Irish
Hill was probably their chief rendezvous.

A rally was made on the following Tuesday, but not extensive
enough to form a ring around any large portion of the forest
where the wolves were supposed to be lurking. Having assembled
at Berlin meeting house, they, however, marched into the woods
and shot two wolves, when they postponed further operations
till the following Saturday, when a grand hunt was proposed in
which all the settlers from the adjoining towns within 20 miles
were to be invited to participate, what they had done being considered merely a reconnaissance.

The assembled forces numbering 400 or 500, then formed themselves into two equal divisions, and chose leaders or captains for
each, with a general officer to remain at the starting point and
give out the order or signal cries to be passed round the ring proposed to be formed. The two captains then led off their respective
divisions, one to the south, along the borders of the woods, and
the other to the west for a short distance and then south, each
leaving a man every 50 or 60 rods, to keep his station till ordered
to march inward, when the ring was completed. After waiting
two hours or more to give time for the divisions to station their
men so as to form an extended ring round the forest proposed to

be enclosed, the word was given out by the general officer, *"Prepare to march."* This was uttered in a loud cry at the starting point, and repeated by the next man left stationed to the south, and soon, if the ring had been perfected by every man, round the ring. In a short time a faint sound was heard on the west side of the ring which grew louder and louder till it reached the starting point in full tone.

All was now animation and expectancy on this part of the ring, and almost instantly the next watchword *"March"* rang through the forest, and each man, as he repeated it, advanced rapidly into the interior of the ring a quarter of a mile as near as he could judge, and then commanded the "halt" as agreed at the outset. This word was promptly sent onward and returned like the others, when another command to march was uttered, and all again advanced towards the supposed center of the ring. And thus rapidly succeeded the watchwords *March* and *Halt*, till the ring was so nearly closed that it was seen and announced that there were enclosed several wolves, in the same, which ran galloping round the centre, as if looking for a chance to escape through the ring, now become a continuous line of men.

But the frightened animals could find no outlets, and were shot down with every attempt to escape. Two wolves and a fox or two were killed in this way, but by this time bullets flew so thickly across the ring that it was seen that some change of plan must be made, else as many men as wolves might be killed. By common consent at this crisis the late Thomas Davis, a well-known marksman and a man of steady nerve was requested to go inside the ring and shoot the wolves. This he did, and accomplished all that was expected of him. He shot five wolves and endangered no man.

The whole number of the victims of the hunt were then found to be seven wolves and ten foxes. The company then took off the scalps of the wolves and took up their line of march for the house of the town clerk, where bounties for the slain wolves were to be allowed and of the avails, some disposition made. It was announced that money to the value adequate had been advanced sufficient to pay for a supper for the whole company. These arrangements were soon effected and while the supper was being cooked a keg of rum was opened and distributed, which being taken in their exhausted condition, on empty stomachs, thus upset a large number who were never so upset before, that it was said that Esquire Knapp's haymow that night lodged a larger number of disabled men than were ever before or since collected in Washington County. DANIEL P. THOMPSON.

Alburg
Grand Isle Co.
Vol. II

Horse-racing was one of the sports with a class, and at intervals became quite exciting. The Iby brothers had a strong-built powerful horse, much noted for his speed; and it was said that he was taken to England, and maintained his reputation there as a turf-horse. An accident occurred about 1830, in a race near Samuel Mott's. On a fourth of July the company had been treated to some racing during the afternoon, when, near night, four horsemen, two from each end of the race-course, happened to start nearly at the same moment, and came rushing on, urging their animals to their utmost speed. Two of the horses passed each other unharmed; the other two struck square, head to head. The riders were both up for dead, but gradually came to, and recovered. Their salvation was owing to the fact, of the horses' heads shooting directly upwards, each rider being prevented from being thrown against his fellow, by his horse's neck. The writer remembers seeing the dead horses lying by the road-side that evening, their necks both broken. Like some of the previously named knock-downs, "rum was at the bottom."

Whitingham
Windham Co.
Vol. V

Gambling and like devices were resorted to for the purpose of raising money for religious and charitable purposes. Churches, roads and bridges were built, repairing loss by fire and paying the State debt, by lottery; clearly showing the tendency of the human mind to be lured by expectation that something is liable to turn up.

These lotteries were not only legalized by towns, but State was concerned in the same demoralizing business.

Vermont has passed 24 acts, granting lotteries for various purposes, the first being dated Feb. 27th, 1783, and the last one, Nov. 8th 1804. Nov. 8th, 1792, an act was passed granting a lottery to raise 150 pounds for building a bridge over Deerfield River at Readsboro.

It was thought that these lotteries had a tendency to relieve the burden of taxation, while it only changed the burden from one class to another by bringing the gamblers to the front in charitable and religious work.

About the time of the commencement of the 19th century there first began to be some religious feeling manifested, and some feeble efforts made to institute Christian worship among the people. A Congregational church was organized about this time, comprising but a limited number as members. Occasional meetings were held in private houses and in barns for several years, but no regular services were held until the church edifice known as the White or Union Church was completed, in 1808. This church was erected to be occupied by the different denominations in proportion as each should hold stock in the same. The original arrangement of this church was a lobby, as it now remains; three aisles on the ground floor; two rows of body pews of square form, seats on all sides; and a single tier of like construction around the outside called wall pews, with a wide gallery on the front and two sides above; and a large elevated pulpit in the extreme back end of the building. No arrangements were made for warming the house, not even a chimney or a place for a stove; and the house was occupied and service held for many years without any warming apparatus.

Shelburne
Chittenden Co.
Vol. 1

The Meeting-House had been built by voluntary subscription, and for nearly thirty years the ministers had been supported in the same manner; the method adopted to raise the sum required being, to assess the same upon the taxlists of those who gave their assent to the contribution. But in March, 1790, an article was inserted in the warning for the town meeting, as follows, viz: "To see if the town will adopt a certain law of this State, entitled *'An act for supporting and maintaining the gospel ministry'*" and at the meeting it passed in the affirmative.

By the act thus adopted, the salary of the ministers was to be assessed upon the polls and ratable estate of the inhabitants of the town, and collected in the same manner as other town taxes; and no person was to be exempt from its payment, unless he lodged with the town clerk for record, the certificate of some minister or officer of another church, that he agreed in religious sentiment with the signer thereof.

This vote created considerable dissatisfaction in the congregation, and Nathan Clark, one of the fathers of the town, denounced it in severe terms, in an article published in the Gazette, over his own signature. The practice thus initiated in 1790, of supporting the ministry by town tax, does not seem to have been abandoned until the repeal of the law on the subject in October, 1807.

The tax for the support of the Minister amounting usually to $150 per annum, appears to have been submitted to with a considerable degree of patience; but the attempt to apply the law to the building of a new meeting-house, which would require more than a ten-fold greater tax, roused a very serious opposition. Those, however, who were in favor of thus erecting the house, were sufficiently strong to carry a vote in the town meeting held December 12, 1803, to raise a tax of 5000 dollars for that purpose.

In 1801 the law providing for the support of the Gospel ministry, and the erection of houses of worship, was so far modified

Old Court-House, Rutland

by the Legislature, that any tax payer could be relieved from contribution, by lodging with the town clerk a certificate signed by
him in the following words, viz: "I do not agree in religious
opinion with a majority of the inhabitants of this town."—And
soon after the vote of the meeting-house tax, the names of 136 of
the payers owning a considerable portion of the property in town,
were found in the clerk's office attached to such a certificate.

We might tell, however, how a certain lawyer by the name of
Richardson, becoming obnoxious to the people, was rode out
of town upon a blacksmith's bellows; as how on another occasion
when the "ardent" had flowed pretty freely, "Old Oliver Perry"
an eccentric and roystering "old bach," washed Landlady Hardy's
cap in the swill-pail and dried it on the gridiron; or how a certain

*Concord
Essex Co.
Vol. I*

justice had his "official dignity" somewhat "damaged" by having
the contents of the landlord's swill-pail poured upon his head
while the pail was placed upon it as he was crowned "*King of
the Swine.*"

Hubbardton Formerly it was the custom for merchants, physicians, &C., to
Rutland Co. deal almost wholly upon trust, and not much matter who they
Vol. III trusted. Their maxim was—trust all, and charge the more, so that
those who pay will make good those who do not. But this, with
their extravagant way of living, occasioned many to fail, and
drove them to the necessity of clearing out, or of taking the poor
debtor's oath, and thus increasing the population of the county
seat. There was much suing in those days and much cost made in
trying to collect bad debts. Attorneys, justices and constables
made it profitable; for, if there was nothing to be obtained of the
debtor, it could be collected of the creditor. The debtor might
go to jail and lie there 40 days and then swear that he was not
worth five dollars more than what the law allowed to each family
—which was their shelter, comfortable furniture and provisions
for the family, one cow, one hog and 10 sheep. And it was said
of those articles, the creditor must make them good; but this part
of the subject was rarely, if ever, enforced.

Fayston In March, 1809, William Newcomb, William Rogers and Marjena
Washington Co. Gardener were elected "hog howards," an office now obsolete,
Vol. IV and exactly what its duties were, even then, we are unable to
learn. But it was an old-time custom to elect newly married men
to that *notable* office, which might have been no sinecure after
all, as the swine in those days all ran where they listed, and unless they were much less vicious than their modern descendants,
it must have needed three "hog constables" to a town to have kept
them in order.

The necessities of the settlers found great relief in making salts *Enosburg* and potash for the northern market. This was almost the only *Franklin Co.* means of obtaining their goods and groceries, and a little money *Vol. II* to meet necessities. The [embargo of 1808] involved this trade in difficulty and danger. Still it seemed a necessity to many, while some, no doubt, practiced contraband for profit. Wind-Mill Point being a port of entry, and the custom officers sustained by an armed posse, under Col. Samuel Page, it became a matter of importance with the smugglers to avoid this port. For this purpose they often crossed from the bottom of Wind-Mill Bay, to the river below, near the Province line, thus flanking the port of entry. A great amount of smuggling has, no doubt, been done, first and last, over this retired road.

It is said that Daniel McGregor, then a resident of Alburgh, but since deceased—a large, active and determined man of Scotch descent—had just entered this road with his load of contraband, when, in the darkness, two armed men from the bushes, one on either side, leaped upon his sleigh. Quick as sight, with a twirl of his loaded whip, he lopped off first one and then the other—his fleet, smuggling roadsters off in a jiffy, leaving, every instant, more distance between him and the muskets of his unknown left-behinds, who, though they fired after him, did him no injury.

The growth of the county experienced another severe check in *Orleans Co.* 1816. That year was memorable as one of extraordinary priva- *Vol. III* tions and sufferings. An unusually early spring had created expectations of a fruitful season and an abundant harvest, but on the morning of June 9th there occurred a frost of almost unprecedented severity, followed by a fall of snow, which covered the earth to the depth of nearly a foot, and was blown into drifts 2 or 3 feet deep. All the growing crops were cut down. Even the foliage on the trees was destroyed, and so completely as respected the beeches, that they did not put forth leaves again that year.

No hope or possibility of a harvest remained, and the settlers had before them the gloomy prospect of extreme scarcity if not of actual famine. Their forebodings were more than realized. Not a single crop came to maturity. Wheat alone progressed so far that by harvesting it while yet in the milk, and drying it in the oven, it might be mashed into dough and baked, or boiled like rice. There was neither corn nor rye except what was brought from abroad, sometimes from a great distance, and at an expense of $3.00 a bushel, and sometimes more. Provisions of every kind were very scarce, and very high. Fresh fish and vegetables of every kind that could possibly be used as food were converted to that purpose. There was extreme sufferings through the summer and fall, and still greater distress during the winter: but it is not known that any one perished by starvation.

At this time, and in fact for a long time before and after, ashes and salts of ashes were about the only commodities which the settlers could exchange for the necessaries of life. The trees fell before the repeated strokes of the axe, were cut into convenient lengths, rolled into heaps and consumed into ashes. These were carefully saved, conveyed to the nearest store, and exchanged for provisions and necessary articles. Many settlers found it expedient to work their ashes into black salts, thus lightening the labor of the transportation. In this form they were conveyed distances of 10 to 20 miles to a market. In some instances, where settlers were too poor to own a team, they have been known to take a bag of salts upon their back to the nearest store.

It was fortunate for these hardy pioneers that pot-ashes always brought a remunerating price in the not remote market of Montreal. Serious inconvenience and probably much actual suffering would have ensued but for this. The little stores in the country towns each had its ashery, and all were eager to purchase.

Upon the sales of their pot and pearl ashes in Montreal they depended almost entirely for the means of remittance to their creditors in the American cities. So important was the traffic that in most of the interior towns of Vermont, during the greater portion of the year, not a dollar in money could be raised, except from the sale of ashes. Without this, goods or provisions could not have been imported, taxes could not have been collected, and the country would have been greatly impeded in its advance and prosperity.

When I was about 12 years of age, the small-pox prevailed in town, and sister Hannah Finney and I were sent to the pest-house which was well filled with patients. Dr. Holton, who afterwards married my sister, was a physician. Hannah was slightly sick— but one eruption filling, and that upon her eyelash. Some of the patients were very sick, and one or two died, especially after the weather became warmer the sickness increased. We all had to get up early, and were not allowed any meat, butter or milk. We were told if we were up early and well starved, when we came to be sick the pits would not fill. To save the scars we starved, and were up in time. *Shrewsbury Rutland Co. Vol. III*

I was repeatedly inoculated while there, but they could not get me down with it, though thin as a skeleton. We hardly ever had anything to eat but dry bread and roast potatoes, without salt. The patients used to send me down to steal salt out of a meat-barrel in the cellar. I would bring it up, and they would wash, dry, and use it. But the Doctor did not know it. He made us take an early morning walk, and a walk in the evening, and we had all kinds of plays but card-playing; blind-man's buff often.

After six weeks, not taking the small-pox, I was dismissed, happy to be released—though I had to diet for two weeks more at home, lest I might yet come down with the disease; and after this, so many stories were told to mother of those who had not taken it in a pest-house, afterwards taking it, and dying with it, back I had to go to my great disgust, and stay another fortnight there, and was put every day to comb a woman's hair whose head was full of scabs. There was nothing to do but to submit to rules and regulations; But do all they could they could not make the small-pox take hold of me. I have escaped to this day.

The old Randall house was used as a pest-house.

Montpelier The third epidemic visiting the town was that fearful disease
Washington Co. known by the name of spotted fever, which, to the general alarm
Vol. IV of the inhabitants, suddenly made its appearance in the village in the Winter of 1811. The first victim was Sibyl Brown, a bright and beautiful daughter of Amasa Brown, of the age of nine years, who, on Saturday, Jan. 2d, was in school, on the evening of that day, sliding with her mates on the ice, and the next morning a corpse. The wife of Aaron Griswold, and the first wife of Jonathan Shepard, were next, and as suddenly destroyed by this terrible epidemic, which struck and swept over the village, and strange to tell, but three deaths of the disease, which at the same time was nearly decimating the then 400 inhabitants of Moretown, and sweeping off 60 or 70 of the 2,000 inhabitants of Woodstock. The chief remedy relied on here was the prompt use of the hot bath, made of a hasty decoction of hemlock boughs; and the pine-board bathing vessel, made in the shape of a coffin, was daily seen, during the height of the disease, in the streets, borne on the shoulders of men, rapidly moving from house to house, to serve in turn the multiplying victims.

Randolph About the year 1800, Dr. Ezekiel Bissell became greatly interested
Orange Co. in the new discovery of vaccination, as a preventive of the dan-
Vol. II gerous and disgusting small-pox. He procured some vaccine mat-
ter from Dr. Morehouse, of Boston. With this he experimented on

his family and such friends as he could persuade to submit to it. Most persons were afraid to trust it, and prejudice against it was strong. The feeling of the people was further aroused by interested efforts of those who made gain by going about the country inoculating all whom they could, and caring for them in what were called "pest-houses." Such a one was established in the house of Judge Storrs.

Dr. Bissell prepared to settle the controversy between him and his opponents. He vaccinated the babe of a woman who had been inoculated for small-pox. In due time the infection showed itself in both cases. The babe with a promising pustule on its arm, but otherwise with its flesh "like the flesh of a little child," lay like a rose on the swollen, discolored bosom of its mother. Multitudes of Randolph people went to see that sight. Near four hundred who had been vaccinated before, were inoculated with virus from the mother, not one of whom experienced any ill result. This settled that controversy.

At that time but little, if anything, was known in regard to the *Brattleboro* proper treatment of insane persons. The faculty were vainly *Windham Co.* groping in the dark for a potent weapon with which they could *Vol. V* meet this mysterious enemy of human happiness called insanity.

A council of physicians—Dr. Marsh of Hinsdale has been mentioned as one of the said council—decided upon trying, for the recovery of Mr. Whitney, a temporary suspension of his consciousness by keeping him completely immersed in water three or four minutes, or until he became insensible, and then resuscitating or awakening him to a new life. Passing through this desperate ordeal, it was hoped, would divert his mind, break the chain of unhappy associations, and thus remove the cause of his disease. Upon trial, this system of regeneration proved of no avail, for, with the returning consciousness of the patient, came the knell of departed hopes, as he exclaimed, "You can't drown love."

According to a former version of the story, there was a second application of the drowning process that terminated the life of Mr. Whitney. But Mr. Hooker, grandson of Rev. Bunker Gay, lately informed us that Mr. Whitney did not pass through a second ordeal by water; the physicians, upon mature deliberations, concluded they were on the right track, but had not used the proper agent for the stupefaction of the life forces. The next and last resort was opium, and Mr. Whitney died under the treatment.

The result of the aforementioned experiments for the cure of insanity may have suggested to the widow of Dr. Marsh, the importance of an asylum for the treatment of that class of persons so afflicted, and thereby her will of $10,000, whence originated the Vermont asylum at Brattleboro.

4

The "Age of Ferment," 1825 to 1860

Caledonia County acknowledged center of Anti-Masonic sentiment, which culminated in election of Governor Palmer on Anti-Masonic ticket in 1831 : Distaste for slavery grew in intensity : Legislature petitioned Congress to deny statehood to any territory permitting slavery : Control of Vermont went to the Republican party, where it has since remained : Religious and temperance fervor high : State-house burned in 1857.

FROM 1832 TO 1840, lectures against slavery met with an unwelcome reception in many towns in New England. Public sentiment as manifested on this subject by the people of Brattleboro, in the Summer of 1837, was more suited to the atmosphere of Hartford, Ct., or Charleston, S.C., than to the free air of Vermont. Looking back 40 years in our history and realizing the comparatively isolated condition and quiet avocations of the people, it is hard to account for the diseased state of the public mind as then exhibited upon this subject. This disease by its malignancy or intensity soon worked its own cure. The conduct of the opponents to these lectures answered their oft repeated question,

Brattleboro Windham Co. Vol. V

"Why do you come *here to lecture* upon slavery, where we have no slaves?"

When ministers of the Gospel refused to read notifications of anti-slavery meetings, when one justice of the peace in Brattleboro advocated the application of tar and feathers to the person of Rev. E. R. Tyler, because he gave lectures upon this subject at the Congregational chapel in Elliot Street, and another justice of the peace said he would "find powder for the mob if they would blow the damned abolitionist down the bank"—we involuntarily became abolitionists. This crusade against free speech, this violation of the right of discussion, as manifested by firing cannons near the windows of the lecture room and loud, disturbing, threatening shouts of a mob—sustained in this rascality, as we knew, by officers of the law and our nearest, and on other subjects, most rational neighbors—convinced thoughtful people that they had a work to do to emancipate themselves.

Such exhibitions of injustice or illiberality, in a community like this, are not without their uses, in the instruction they convey to perpetrators as well as the victims of it. Probably this place is now as free from public intolerance as any community in the world. There is ample proof that persecution, whether from combinations of men or individuals, is beneficial to the persecuted. In the Autumn of 1842 a stone was thrown against the door of the Methodist chapel, in Canal Street, while a Second Advent preacher was on his knees at prayer; he exclaimed instantly, "God bless that stone."

FUGITIVE'S DIRECTORY—*Impromptu.*

By Samuel Goss.

Montpelier Washington Co. Vol. IV

Old Gov. Wise is all in a foam
Because his black cattle to Northern States roam,
And bids us poor Yankees to send them all back,
Without e'en a bloodhound to scent out their track.

But humanity says, No, let them rest here a while,
And their fears of re-capture in slumbers beguile.
But when they resolve to quit the straw as their bed,
Just stuff their old pockets with dried beef and bread,
And bid them go forward alone, in the night,
With the star in the north as their guide and their light,
To degree 45 near the line of the State,
And the beautiful plain of Canada East,
Where prudence suggests a permanent stand,
Quite removed from the lash of the slave-driver's hand.
And here let them rest, and effectually prove,
The obvious fact—a pleasant remove.

In 1842, Mr. Camp also introduced, at the church meeting, the *Derby* following resolutions in regard to slavery, and they were unan- *Orleans Co.* imously adopted: *Vol. III*

"*Whereas* the sin of holding our fellow men in bondage, as exhibited in the Southern States, is now generally acknowledged and deplored by all well informed Christians, and also that the guilt of participation attached to them so far as they fail to bear decided testimony against it; and whereas, in conformity with the principle involved in the command, 'Thou shalt not suffer sin upon thy neighbor,' every Christian becomes to a certain extent the keeper of every brother Christian, and is bound, faithfully, but kindly, to tell him of his faults; therefore:

"*Resolved*, That professing Christians who hold their fellow-men in such bondage incur the guilt of violating the law of God —And however in some ages of the world this may have been winked at, all men in this county have now the means of full information and though they may be ignorant, are entirely without excuse.

"*Resolved*, That while we respect and love our brethren, Christian charity does not require our Christian faithfulness permit to cover over or palliate their faults.

"*Resolved*, That this church cannot hold in fellowship those who practice, excuse or tolerate the sin of slavery, nor justify them in coming to the table of the Lord, pretending to obey His commands; and if such profess to be ministers of the Gospel, we cannot admit them to our pulpit as Christian teachers.

"*Resolved*, That we hold it to be the duty of bodies of associated ministers and private Christians of all denominations in the free States and elsewhere, kindly, but faithfully, to admonish those of the slave States, clearly point out their danger, and urge them to repentance."

St. Albans Franklin Co. Vol. II The legislature of Vermont, Oct. 30, 1844, repealed every act in relation to the militia, thus abolishing all military organizations and trainings, and leaving the State with no defence against foreign aggression, or force to secure internal tranquility. The martial spirit of the people was not merely allowed to decline, but through the example of our law-makers, was made the subject of idle jest and ridicule. The officers, whose military consequence was thus summarily destroyed, were more or less indignant; but the rank and file, who had long since voted June training a bore, were well pleased. The noisy drum and ear-piercing fife were silenced, banners were furled, and plumes went drooping. Swords and guns were put aside to rust and corrode, and dashy uniforms were packed away to become the pasturage of moths.

But June training was not thus to pass into oblivion. From the shades of Academus were to come the men, who, for a time at least, were to preserve its memory in vivid recollection. Overturned by our law-makers it might be; but it was yet to become a subject of profound and earnest agitation in college halls, and to furnish matter for grave and anxious deliberation to the erudite and reverend savants. The students of the University at Burlington (or perhaps I should say a large proportion of them) combined to honor the memory by a fantastical celebration of the first Tuesday in June.

University of Vermont

On each returning anniversary a grotesque procession was formed in which a variety of characters and professions were represented. Proceeding from the college campus, they marched through the principal streets. The music of the occasion was furnished by drums and fifes to the hands of those who never handled a musical instrument before. To these were added a band made up of obsolete instruments of tin and brass—the sackbut, psaltery, dulcimer and shawm—tang-lang, locofodies and hugag. On arriving at the court-house square, they drew up in front of the American hotel, where spectators had congregated to the number of two or three thousand. Here they were reviewed by the commander-in-chief, Col. Jefferson Brick, who delivered an appropriate speech. After a salute of one gun by the flying artillery, from a toy cannon of half-inch calibre, and closed in sundry joints of rusty stove-pipe and drawn by 8 specimens of skin and bones once known as horses, the corps returned to the college, where they were disbanded.

"We have discovered in a majority of schools, a want of thoroughness. Scholars are too much confined to text-books, and, although they may answer verbally every question as it is in the book, they may know nothing of the lesson. In one school, after a scholar had recited perfectly all the definitions of the different angles and triangles, I asked her to make a right angle on the board, but she had no more idea of a right angle than she had of the conjugation of a Greek verb. In another school, a class that had recited a perfect lesson in geography, could neither bound nor give the name of this town. Some, after having been through their geographies, cannot tell whether the equator divides the earth into northern and southern, or eastern and western hemispheres. Deplorable ignorance!—showing a deficiency somewhere, either in parent, scholar, or teacher; probably in all three.

"Was it so with those of us who obtained our limited educa-

Fairlee
Orange Co.
Vol. II

tion, half a century or more ago? So far as the writer is aware, it was not. Then, what little we learned, we learned well—we were drilled in Webster's until we had it by heart—the teacher daily asking a thousand and one questions, or less, that no author ever thought of publishing in a book; but all useful to a thorough drilling of the pupil. Soon we were permitted to try our hand at penmanship, and our teachers were not above giving instructions in that important branch of an education, as some at the present day are, who say it is a separate and distinct branch of education, to be taught exclusively by a writing-master. In looking over the school registers in the different districts in town, we find that only about one in ten of the inhabitants of the town have visited any of the schools, during the past year.

"We think these figures indicate a lack of interest in the schools! If there is anything that will encourage a teacher, stimulate the scholars to a more active pursuit of study, and promote a more general interest withal—it is to receive frequent visits from the inhabitants and friends who are interested in the work. And we would suggest and earnestly recommend to the people of every school district, who never saw the inside of their school-house more than once a year, to make the pilgrimage from their homes to their school-house, and visit their school four times each year. If every family in each school district was actively engaged in the prosperity and success of our schools, and directed their most earnest efforts to the accomplishment of that end, our schools would be far more successful, and the rising generation would grow up to tread the higher walks of an educated life, rather than walk the careless paths of the half-educated—hardly ever rising above the dead level of the world."

Middlesex "Uncle Daniel Vaughn," as he was universally called in Windsor
Washington Co. County, was a man about 5 feet, 10 inches in height, broad
Vol. IV shouldered, stout built, and weighing some more than 200 pounds.

He was noted for his remarkable strength, his strong, heavy voice, his sociability, his song-singing and story-telling, and was a notedly robust man, the solidity of muscle increasing as age advanced to such an extent as to make it necessary for him to use a cane or crutches for the last 15 years of his life.

He died of dropsy June 3, 1846, aged 78 years, and by his request was buried in a place selected by himself in a sightly spot near the house where he died. The following March the eldest daughter of James Vaughn, aged 16, died of consumption, and was buried in a grave near her grandfather. In February 1855 their remains were taken up to be removed to the family burying-lot in Woodstock cemetery. The remains of the young lady were found in the usual condition of those buried that length of time.

The uncommon heft of Mr. Vaughn's coffin led to an examination of the remains, when it was found that the body had become petrified. Every part, excepting the nose, was in perfect form, nearly its natural color, but a little more of a yellowish tinge, hard like stone, and it weighed 550 pounds. The petrified body was viewed by Mr. Vaughn's family and many of the neighbors in Middlesex, and was also seen by many at Woodstock. A somewhat minute examination by physicians and scientific men revealed the fact that the fingers, toes and the outer part of the body were very hard and brittle, but that the length of time had not been sufficient to so fully change the inner portions of the most fleshly parts of the body and limbs. But it was generally believed by those who made examination that a few years more of time would have made the work of petrification complete, and changed the entire body to a mineral formation, that would perhaps endure for ages.

Jan. 6, 1857, the State House, which was being warmed up on the eve of the septenary Constitutional Convention, caught fire from the furnace, and all but the empty granite walls, with their brick

Montpelier Washington Co. Vol. IV

linings, was destroyed, and all the contents, except the library, which was got out, and the books and papers in the safe of the Secretary of State's office, a few articles of furniture and the portrait of Washington, was reduced to a heap of ruins.

Burning of the State House.

By Joseph A. Wing, Esq.

O'er Montpelier, beauteous town,
The shades of night were closing down;
The lovely moon, the queen of night,
Was driving on her chariot bright;
And star on star their influence lent,
'Til glowed with fire the firmament,
The wind was blowing high and strong,
And swept in fearful gusts along;
The piercing cold had cleared the street
Of merry voice and busy feet,—
And gathered 'round the cheerful hearth,
The smiling face, the social mirth,
Show'd that the night was gaily past,
While outward howled the roaring blast.

What means that wild and startling cry,
To which the echoing hills reply?
First feeble, low, and faint and mild;
Then loud, and terrible and wild.
'Tis fire! fire! that awful sound!
Fire! fire! fire! the hills resound!
Now rising near—now heard afar,
The stillness of the night to mar,
Join'd with the wind's wild roaring, hear
The cry of fire burst on the ear!
Forth from the hearth, the shop, the store,
At that dread sound, the myriads pour—
And, gathering as they pass along,

Each street and alley swells the throng,
The rattling engines passing by,
The roaring wind, the larum cry,
The ringing bells, the wild affright,
Still add new terrors to the night.

See yonder grand and stately pile,
With lofty dome, and beauteous aisle,
Our village glory and our pride,
Whose granite walls old Time defied;
Her halls of state, her works of art,
Both please the eye, and charm the heart.

The wind roars loud, the flames flash high,
Leaping and dancing to the sky;
    While in the rooms below,
From hall to hall resistless rushing,
From doors and windows furious gushing—
    Oh! how sublime the show!

Roar on, fierce flame; beneath thy power
The works of years, in one short hour,
    Are swept from earth away;
And nought is left of all their pride,
But ashes, scattered far and wide,
And crumbling walls, with smoke dark-dyed
    Spread out in disarray.

That lofty pile, one hour ago—
The State's just pride, the Nation's show,
Capp'd with its bright and virgin snow—
    In beauty shone:
The next, a mass of ruined walls,
Of columns broke, and burning halls—
    Its beauty flown.

Pawlet   Before 1812, there were but few, if any, fine-wooled sheep in
Rutland Co.   town. About that time Col. Humphreys, of Connecticut, brought
Vol. III   here a few choice sheep, descended from his original importation
in 1802. The obstructions to commerce during the times of the
embargo and the war with England in 1812, had induced the
establishment of woolen-factories in this town, and throughout
the county, and a finer grade was in demand. Merino sheep were
soon diffused throughout the town, and a new era in sheep breed-
ing was inaugurated. Wool soon became a principal staple.

About 1825, Saxony sheep were brought in and crossed with
Merino grades. This did not prove satisfactory, as tenderer sheep
and lighter fleeces were the result. To counteract this the Bake-
well breed was soon after introduced, which gave less satisfaction.
During all these earlier efforts to improve sheep, but few people
attempted to raise pure-blooded sheep, but our highest ambition
was satisfied with grade sheep. During the present decade a new
impulse has been given to the sheep interest by the introduction
of the improved American Merino. The key-note to this last
movement has been full-bloods.

A few prime flocks of this class have been started in town. The
wool-growing interest has been depressed for the last year or two,
and our shepherds have wished themselves out of the business.
New encouragement, however, has been afforded them by an
Act of Congress, passed in March 1867, increasing the tariff on
imported wool.

Shelburne   Justices were almost universally employed to perform the mar-
Chittenden Co.   riage ceremony, and the marriage fee was one dollar; and the
Vol. 1   officiating magistrate was considered very penurious if he did not
make a present of that dollar to the bride; and in many cases an

amount of flax was purchased with that dollar and manufactured into linen for family use—hetcheled, carded, spun and in some instances woven with her own hands. Household or domestic labor was not considered derogatory, and a calico dress was a respectable marriage outfit. I recollect in one instance, in performing the marriage ceremony the justice and the father of the bride having a relish for gin and having imbibed freely of that cordial previous to the ceremony, when the happy couple presented themselves ready for the ceremony with their gloves on, the justice required them to remove their gloves, as his custom was to marry *skin to skin*.

Fashions and ceremonies have materially changed. It would not be considered respectable at the present time to have a marriage solemnized by a justice. These rites must be performed by the pastor or some noted clergyman, and $10 dollars is considered a moderate marriage fee. A notable change also has been gradually manifesting itself in regard to families. Most of the early settlers had families numbering from 8 to 15 children, and in some cases even more. John Hadley's family numbered 25 children, Benjamin Sutton's 24, Ebenezer Barstow's 13, and many other families from 10 to 15 children. From 1810 to 1825 the school-houses in every part of the town were filled with scholars, numbering from 50 to 100 in each district. But at the present time, in several districts, barely a sufficient number for a small class can now be gathered.

No state criminals, and only five college graduates, viz: Elon Olds Martin, afterwards settled as Presbyterian minister in Lowndes County, Ala.; Charles Parker, who is at present a Congregational minister in Vermont; William Richmond, late principal of St. Albans high school, St. Albans; Henry Thorp, now in the state of Oregon; and Gay H. Naramore. These are all that graduated in due course. *Underhill Chittenden Co. Vol. 1*

TEMPERANCE

Enosburg Like other towns, this took the alarm and instituted a Temperance
Franklin Co. Society. Most of our prominent men signed the pledge of total
Vol. II abstinence, and organized by choosing David I. Farnham, Pres't,
Austin Fuller, V.P. &C. Farnham was a young lawyer just commenced practicing in town. Having never had such a dignitary,
we were disposed to pay him all due respect. Soon it was whis-
pered around that the president had been drinking—in fact that
he had drank the night he was chosen to office. A meeting was
called to see what to do about it, the vice-president taking the
chair. In their haste, and honesty too, the society had neglected
to frame by-laws, and, of course, could now make none to reach
the case. Mr. F., after listening awhile, and seeing their dilemma,
arose and said he would be glad to help them "get rid of a bad
penny, but saw no way to do it"; and, by way of apology for
what was charged against him, said he was sincere in joining them
as he did, having drank just before he left the tavern—his board-
ing-place—and did not feel as though he should want to drink
again; but on getting home "felt differently, and of course drank";
and closed his remarks by saying his being elected to office "was
not a matter of his, at all." Meeting broke up in no good humor.

Gov. Eaton, then a young man whose whole soul was in the
work, drafted the constitution of "The Enosburgh Young Men's
Temperance Society" [since altered to "Total Abstinence Society"—A.M.H., Ed.] limiting the age of the leading offices to 30
years, but all ages joined. The young lawyer soon left, and we
have not been blest much with lawyers since. The longest unbroken history is claimed for this organization in the State.

Cabot About 1823, the farmers began to think raising so many potatoes
Washington Co. was running out their farms, and, after all, not so profitable as
Vol. IV some other crops, and less were planted; and the number of dis-

tilleries decreased until, in 1832, there were none running in town, and New England rum was used by those who thought they must have something stimulating, and sold freely at all the stores and hotels in town.

About 1825, the temperance question began to be agitated; people commenced to think they could get along without quite so much stimulant, and from that time to the present, there has been a marked diminution in the quantity absorbed in town.

The writer has in this matter endeavored to state facts simply and fully, but does not mean to be understood as saying that in the manufacture and sale of liquors, Cabot was a sinner above the other towns in that vicinity, for it is probably a fact that for its number of inhabitants, it had fewer distilleries than any other town in this section.

In 1826, Samuel Kendall, having a quantity of grain for which at that time there was no market, built a distillery and worked the grain into whiskey; and after running it about 2 years, one morning when going to the distillery, he saw a poor man coming towards him with a half bushel of corn on his back, and when the man came to the road that turned down to the distillery, he stopped and looked towards the distillery, then started toward the grist-mill, then stopped and seemed deliberating whether he should go to the mill and get his corn ground for his half-famishing children, or whether he should go to the distillery and sell his corn for whiskey, till finally his greater appetite for whiskey overbalanced his better judgment, and had won the contest. He then turned with his small measure of corn and went to the distillery, and sold his corn for whiskey. On arriving at the distillery, Samuel Kendall asked his brother (who was running the distillery at this time in company with him): "Have you emptied that man's corn from the bag?" On the brother answering that he had, he re-

Enosburg
Franklin Co.
Vol. II

quested him to put it back in the bag and then told his brother that he would sell no more whiskey in small quantities.

Underhill
Chittenden Co.
Vol. 1

Lawyers have never thrived in this locality. Cheese-making or horse-raising is usually esteemed more honorable as well as lucrative.

In the year 1821, however, a young man by the name of Bacon tried to practice law here for a short time, but gave it up soon and has not been heard of since. A firm of Sawyer & Beardsley stayed longer, but were not successful.

LITTLE HOUSEHOLD PET

By Mrs. Emily J. Colby.

Sutton
Caledonia Co.
Vol. 1

In the spring time, low, we laid her,
    Darling, little, household pet,
And our hearts are filled with anguish
    And our eyes with tears are wet.

Yes, we miss her, sadly miss her
    In the parlor, in the hall;
Oft we stop and listen, listen
    For her merry voice to call.

Can the angels need the children
    On that bright, celestial plain?
Is the heavenly music sweeter
    That they join the glad refrain?

Perhaps the Father saw our need
    And to draw our hearts to Him
Took our treasure up to Heaven,
    That we might long to enter there.

Brattleboro

Oft we hear our darling's voice
    Sweetly calling, "Father, come!
Father, mother, meet your children
    In this bright, celestial home."

The year 1840 will ever associate with its recollection, all the *Alburg* excesses of the Harrison campaign log cabins, coon skins, hard *Grand Isle Co.* cider, and song-singing. The Temperance reform had previous to *Vol. II* this taken strong hold in the community, but the excessive political excitement of this election, like a sweeping tornado, for the time seemed to carry almost every thing before it. It became apparent soon afterward to the friends of Temperance, that something must be done in the line of reform and repairs, and accordingly in the winter of 1841–2 they commenced and continued a series of meetings in the different school districts throughout the town, delivering spirited addresses, and also laying music, as in the political campaign, under contribution, in the shape of suitable selections and some original pieces, awakening much interest. Many united who had hitherto stood aloof; a committee was appointed to visit the liquor-sellers in the town and endeavor to dissuade them from the continuance of the practice, which was productive of much good, and the discipline of the society was thoroughly enforced.

It is with pleasure we recall that sunny day of his long life among *Brattleboro* us, in the summer of 1840, when the oak grove in the rear of Col. *Windham Co.* Joseph Goodhue's residence was honored by the presence of *Vol. V* Daniel Webster, who there gave a short address to the people of this place. The long cavalcade of citizens for escort duty, the expression upon each face, the elastic step of youth and age, with other indications, told us Brattleboro was proud that day.

Hope for a season bade the whigs farewell, for, since the election of John Q. Adams, in 1824, they had up to this time, been unsuccessful in every Presidential contest.

The great political revival of this year was of such a character as heralded success. The political prospect not only gave great pleasure to our venerable friend, but also to a large majority of the people in this town. All seemed to appreciate the privilege of seeing this oracle of the party, whose fame had gone around the globe—that great Daniel, who, on the floor of Congress, had shut the lion's mouth as it was about to close upon the blood-bought constitution of 1787.

When Mr. Webster was seated upon the platform erected in the grove, Judge Whitney instantly threw off his hat, and renewed vigor came to that time-worn frame and face, as, with clear untrembling voice, he loudly exclaimed: "*Ladies and Gentlemen: The Defender of the Constitution.*"

It was enough. Surely nothing could be said more fitting the occasion.

Montpelier Location of the *Vermont Patriot*: Westerly side of Main Street,
Washington Co. opposite Bethany Church; wood structure; printing-office in the
Vol. IV second story; rear part of first story occupied as a book-bindery by a Mr. Watson, who went to South Carolina and died there, and the front part for the post-office, kept by Mr. Hill. When the southern and western mails arrived, by stage—about the same time, 10 to 11 o'clock, A.M.—the little room would be crowded to excess. After the mail was opened, Postmaster Hill would read out in a loud voice the address of every letter received, upon the conclusion of which there would be a stampede of those for whom there were no letters.

The *Patriot* was published here until it passed into the hands of Marston & Barker, when it was removed to State Street, in the Ballou building, opposite First National Bank, where the printing-office was in the second story, Mr. Marston having a book-store on the first floor, and a large reading-room, well supplied with newspapers, in the rear, for the benefit of anyone who chose to use it.

It was there the friends of the editor and *Patriot* gathered for news and political gossip. It was in this room the election of James K. Polk was first announced in Montpelier by a hurried scrawl from Hon. J. McM. Shafter, then Whig Secretary of State for Vermont, written at Burlington and forwarded by the stage-driver to Col. E. P. Jewett, it reading as follows: "New York gone! all gone! We have got to take Polk, Texas and the devil!" And we also got with Polk that vast and rich territory comprising not only Texas, but New Mexico, Utah, Arizona, Nevada and California.

In 1848 the Free Soil party became somewhat popular in this place. The Democrats and Abolitionists uniting as Free Soilers, nominated as their candidate Henry S. Morse, who had for several years been the nominee of the Democratic party, and elected him over Mr. Root the Whig candidate for re-election. A strife for the next year soon commenced, intended at first to be carried on privately, but soon became open and general by both parties, and was carried to extremes. Votes were bought, and men were bribed in every way possible; money was freely and largely offered. The whole country was ransacked for absent voters who had not lost their residence by limitation. Foreigners of all nations and tongues were naturalized by both parties; and many kept under guard, as it were, for months previous to election day.

Shelburne Chittenden Co. Vol. I

Individuals hired by one party and their families supported, mysteriously disappeared a short time before election. Laboring men were kept in employ through the season who were unprofitable, in order to secure their votes. In brief, no means was left untried or unused by either party that could secure a vote; and no means however dishonorable were resorted to by one party, which the other party was not guilty of. But election day came, and the contest was a scrutinizing one. Legal advisers were employed on either side to attend the examination of voters. Almost every voter had to pass a scrutinizing examination; and it was late in the evening before the examination was closed.

When all had voted, the box was taken by the authority to a side apartment away from the multitude that thronged the town room, and none admitted but those qualified by law. Many had come from adjoining towns to learn the results. Both parties had their hopes and fears. The result of the balloting was such that the multitude was kept in anxious suspense for some time—there being 107 for Mr. Morse, 104 for Mr. Root, 2 scattering, and 3 blanks or pieces of newspaper. Some of the Root party contended strongly that those 3 blanks must be counted as scattering votes—which would constitute no choice. Others contended that blanks could not be deemed votes and should not be counted, and that Mr. Morse was elected.

A warm debate was held for some time, and at one time a personal encounter was imminent. But the question was finally referred to Mr. Adams, who had retired from the town room. He was sent for; and on entering, the question was put to him: "Do blank votes count?" Not knowing how the case stood, he promptly answered "No"; which decided the case in favor of Mr. Morse, which was heralded to the anxious multitude—kept for a long time in suspense—and caused a shout of triumph from the Free Soil party, and an almost instant disappearance of the Whig party. It is earnestly hoped that another like contest will never occur.

Stowe
Lamoille Co.
Vol. II
Some slight traces of gold have been found in many localities in town, especially on the small streams—more, perhaps, upon what is called "Gold Brook" than anywhere else. In May 1857, Capt.

A. H. Slayton, who had previously had considerable experience in the diggings of California, discovered some small particles of gold on the banks of that brook, on the farm then owned by Nathaniel Russell, Esq. In the following November, he purchased the farm and commenced digging, employing three or four hands several days. It is presumed that he did not find the shining metal in sufficient abundance to make it pay well, or he would have continued operations, which he did not do, but he took out sufficient to make a splendid watch-chain worth about $100, and several other persons have specimens of jewelry manufactured from gold taken out by him, and found in other places.

POST-OFFICE

There was no public mail service in Cabot till 1808. The only newspaper taken by the pioneer settlers was the *North Star*, then as now published at Danville, and this was procured by each subscriber taking his turn in sending his boy, or going himself on horseback to the printing office, and bringing the papers for his neighborhood in saddle-bags. What he could not distribute on his way home were left at the grist-mill, then owned and run by Thomas Lyford, on the same site where the mill now stands, and by him were distributed as the subscribers came, or sent to the mill for them. None of the subscribers of that day are now living, but their children tell me that the receipt of the paper was deemed a matter of so much importance that all the family gave attention while some one of their number, by the light of the tallow candle or the fainter flicker of the fireplace, read aloud not only the news but the entire contents of the paper.

*Cabot
Washington Co.
Vol. IV*

Letters were brought by travelers passing through the town. In this way the early settlers received their mails for the first 23 years.

Chief among the early missionaries in Washington County and in Montpelier, was Lorenzo Dow, a Methodist preacher; not a conference preacher, exactly, but one whose circuit extended all over Vermont, the Canadas, the South, Ireland, Scotland, and wherever he chose to go; who came and went as the "wind that bloweth wherever it listeth." A true, genuine Methodist, though; he never preached any other doctrine. The pioneer of Methodism in Washington County but a man who must be his own leader, who could never restrain himself to circuit rules. He had joined the Methodist Conference in his youth, had been appointed to a circuit; it could not hold him; remonstrated with, reappointed, shot off on a fervent tangent. Conference dropped him, could not keep a man it could neither rule or guide.

Dow often said on parting with his audience, "One year from this day, I will again preach here." The people, after he left, laughed at his giving out an appointment so far ahead and at his supposing that he would keep it. The year came round, no one remembered it, but, Lo! in a year to the day and hour, Dow appeared to fulfill his engagement; his first salutation to the crowd, gathering around him, "Crazy Dow is with you once again!" He preached as I never heard any one but him, for three hours he held his large audience so still you could have heard a pin drop on the floor, said our narrator, and at the end of his sermon, gave out another appointment for a year from the day. People rather looked for him the next year.

In Vermont, in passing through a dense woods one day to fill an appointment, he saw two men chopping wood. He mounted on a large stump, and said "Crazy Dow will preach from this stump 6 months from today, at 2 o'clock, P.M." Six months from that time an immense audience was assembled, and Dow in going to the place saw a man in great distress looking for something. Dow inquired what the matter was. The man replied that he was poor, and that someone had stolen his axe, and that he felt the loss very much. Lorenzo told him if he would go to the meeting he would find his axe. Before getting to the place of service, Dow picked up a stone and put it in his pocket. After the delivery of a powerful sermon, Dow said, "There is a man here who has had his axe stolen, and the thief is here in this audience, and I am going to throw this stone right to his head," drawing back his hand as though in the act of throwing the stone. One man ducked his head. Dow went up to him and said, "You have got this man's axe!" And so he had, and went and brought it and gave it to him.

DONATION FESTIVALS

were introduced about 1830, and have become very popular. In their inception they were limited to the supply of the pastorate with such necessary articles as each donor could conveniently spare from his own stores, and subserved two principal objects: providing additional aid to the frequently scanty resources of the pastorate, and bringing into special relations the people of the parish so apt to form into cliques and classes having little or no sympathy with each other. We cannot doubt their effect has been to create more sympathy among the people, and between the pastor and people, to say nothing of the material aid furnished the pastor.

Pawlet Rutland Co. Vol. III

These festivals are now brought into requisition to aid any unfortunate member of society, who, by sickness, or accident, stands in need of help, and also used to raise funds for benevolent purposes and special public objects. Through their agency here and elsewhere, churches and parsonages have been furnished; cemeteries bought, enclosed, and improved; hospital stores collected for the army; soldiers' monuments erected, and Sabbath school and other public libraries established. And since money has become the most plentiful article in the community, donations are almost exclusively made in cash, and not infrequently from $100 to $200 are raised in an evening. They have become the festival of the day, and whatever the object, seldom fail to call out a crowd.

Albany
Orleans Co.
Vol. III
There are also, in the east part of this town, the Catholics—this people so peculiar in their habits—and they have a strong hold upon some of the best farms in the eastern and central parts of town; and last year they commenced to build a church. They have the house up, and the out-side finished; and the priest tells them when they pay in full for that, he will cause the inside to be completed, which will probably be accomplished this present year, 1870. A more thrifty or industrious class of people, perhaps, cannot be found in town; and with a few exceptions, they are "dacent" people, and most of the families take pains to send their children to school, though I am sorry to say some do not.

Brookfield
Orleans Co.
Vol. III
One of the earliest settlers on the tract now called Bradford, was a religious fanatic by the name of Benoni Wright, who conceived it to be his privilege and duty to prepare himself for the distinguished honor and service pertaining to a prophet of the Lord, by letting his beard grow to a great length, and by keeping a strict fast of forty days and nights in the wilderness, devoting the time to meditation and fervent prayer. When about to retire, he prepared himself with a leathern girdle with a buckle on one end and forty progressive holds in the other, designing to gird himself, day by day, one degree closer as his size should diminish. For this purpose it is said he took up his abode in the cave above mentioned.

This process went on till the imperious demands of appetite became too strong for his resolution and in the darkness of night he was detected far away from his place of concealment, in quest of food to satisfy his hunger, for if he stayed where he had intended to remain, he was convinced he must die; and so his sanctimonious attempt proved a ridiculous failure. Still he immortalized himself, as his name has been permanently attached to the mountain which witnessed his effort so painful, to become a distinguished prophet of the Most High. Let the place of his retirement be also called by his name—*Wright's Cave*.

In the Fall or early Winter of 1842 a man by the name of Chandler, a preacher, came to Jamaica, and wished to lecture on the second coming of Christ as declared by Miller. He proposed to show from the prophecies that the end would come on a certain month and day in 1843, and, being an eloquent speaker and able reasoner, many very soon embraced his views. Great excitement prevailed. Other preachers of the same faith soon arrived, and this excitement lasted during the next summer and autumn. Farmers neglected their fields, alleging that the world would end before harvest, and crops that had matured were left to waste. Meetings were held in different places almost continually, till people were exhausted by fatigue, anxiety and want of sleep. *Jamaica Windham Co. Vol. V*

A company of these fanatics collected at the house of a Mr. Young in the south part of the town. The house was thronged day after day until the community became alarmed for the health and reason of those in attendance. The civil authority visited them and in kindness requested that they stop the meetings for a time and get rest and sleep, but all to no purpose. A few days after this, Mrs. Young died from over-excitement.

A Mrs. Stocker in the same neighborhood became insane and committed suicide, while many others appeared for the time to have lost their reason. Property was wasted, families neglected and churches rent in pieces. Finally, upon setting time after time for the second advent, and being as often disappointed, many acknowledged their mistake and the excitement abated. "God grant," says an eye-witness, "that we may never see the like again."

Brattleboro
Windham Co.
Vol. V
In those days, when every minister's house was regarded as an inn or refectory by every other minister, whether known or unknown, who wanted rest or refreshment, a young man called upon Dr. Well. Soon after the introduction, a dialogue ensued much like the following:

Stranger. "Are there any heresies among you?"

Dr. W. "I know not whether I understand the drift of your question."

Stranger. "I wish to inquire, Sir, whether there be any Armenians, Socinians, or Universalists among you?"

Dr. W. "Oh, Sir, there are worse heretics than any of these."

Stranger. "My dear Sir, what can be worse?"

Dr. W. "Why, there are some who get drunk, and some who quarrel with their families, or their neighbors, and some who will not pay their debts when they might do it, and some who are very profane. Such men I think far worse heretics than those for whom you inquire."

Bakersfield
Franklin Co.
Vol. II
The first house of worship of the Congregational church was dedicated March 1831. In 1850 they removed to the house that now stands upon the common. The church has the following records in regard to vain amusements and the subjects of Temperance:

"*Resolved, 1st* (1839)—That we will restrain our domestics and children, so far as practicable, from attendance on vain amusements.

"*Resolved, 2d*—That we will observe the Sabbath day, by doing no more than what is implied in leading the colt to water, or pulling the ox out of the pit."

Traveling on the Sabbath was also defined as a disciplinable offence.

In 1844 it was voted to receive hereafter into the church no person by profession or letter, who habitually uses or sells intoxicating liquors as a beverage. There is no record of any action upon the subject of slavery. But various members of the church were among the earliest and most earnest anti-slavery men.

L. G. Mead, Jr., early manifested a taste for drawing and sculpture. His frequent copies from nature on paper canvas, and in marble, during his clerkship with Messrs. Williston & Tyler in 1853, caused his friends to think he would not long remain behind the counter selling nails, paint and putty. His local fame attracted the attention of that well-known artist, Henry K. Brown, while on a short visit to this place in the summer of 1853. Two favored sons of genius met. The claims of the younger to favorable consideration being honored by the elder, an artist of established reputation and old world experience, probably decided the pathway of the younger for life. The decisive step was taken by placing himself under the instructions of Mr. Brown at New York, where the young aspirant diligently improved his favorable opportunities about two years, when he returned to his home at Brattleboro, in December 1856, where he soon gave evidence of his progress in art by a New Year's freak.

Brattleboro Windham Co. Vol. V

On the last night of the old year, assisted by a comrade, with snow and water, he constructed an image, called the "Recording Angel." The occasional applications of water, during the progress of the work, made the snow more susceptible to manipulation and gave the whole figure greater hardness and solidity, as the night was so cold each application of water soon became solid. Standing in a snow bank in a freezing atmosphere with a lantern "dimly burning," or "the moonbeams' misty light," would be more favorable conditions for the burial of Sir John Moore than for the exercise of genius in the work proposed. Conveniently near the scene of operations, at the joining of the two roads at North Main Street, was John Burnham's old foundry building. Access was gained thereto, at the midnight hour, and a sufficient quantity of snow carried into a warmer atmosphere, where were formed the most expressive parts of the figure, in the north room of that old building. We will give, in his own language, the account of a noted citizen of this place, on this occasion:

"As morning dawned, there, at a fork of the two principal streets of the village, stood an image, bright in the rays of the morning sun, and brighter still with the magic light of genius. The mischievous boy stood appalled by the unwonted sight; it was surely no idle work for him to cast his snowballs at. A noted simpleton of the village, after looking at it for a moment, ran away from it in fear and alarm, and a man who rarely ever before made a bow, raised his hat in respect."

This figure remained in perfection over two weeks, unprotected save by the sanctity of genius. New York papers gave an account of this affair, and a resident of Brattleboro, when off the coast of Chili, heard a sea captain read the account from a Spanish paper.

Soon after this event Mr. Mead received several commissions: one from Nicholas Longworth, Esq., of Cincinnati, for a duplicate of the snow statue in marble, and one from Richards Bradley, for a marble bust of his grandfather, Hon. William C. Bradley. A full-length colossal statue of Ethan Allen was made by him for the State of Vermont, and is now in the State House at Montpelier. Rev. Edward Atwater, of New Haven, then recently from Europe, and some parties in New Orleans gave him commissions, all of which he executed to the satisfaction of the applicants, previous to his departure for Florence, Italy. The last accounts of him from that place are a hopeful character for his world-wide fame.

RAIL ROAD.

Bolton
Chittenden Co.
Vol. 1
The building of the Vermont Central Rail Road through Bolton, was an event that is worthy of notice. The rocks were very hard

to work and therefore it required great expense to grade the road through this town. It was commenced in the Spring of 1847, by making two temporary settlements of Irish, one containing 100, and the other 200, inhabitants. Suel Belknap contracted the building of the road from Montpelier to Burlington, and this portion was underlet to Barker and others. The work went on lively for two or three months, when discontent began to spread among the laborers, on account of not being paid for their work, and the "patch" was soon in a state of general insurrection after the fashion of the "ould country."

The upper settlement was nicknamed *Cork*, and the lower, *Dublin*. They surrounded R. Jones's hotel day and night, and demanded their "pay" of Mr. Barker and others who were boarding there, or they would take their lives. Noisy Irishmen would mount one at a time on carts or barrels, and deliver furious specimens of "Irish eloquence" to the excited crowd, about "hard work," "want of provisions," "no money," "worse than highway robbery," "miserable vagabonds cheating poor honest men out of their pay." Then there would be a murmur of applause, and some would say " 'nd ye spake well." While the women ran to and fro with their wide cap borders fluttering, arms gesticulating, and tongues going like flutter wheels.

> "Much was the noise, the clamor much
> Of men, and boys and dogs."

Yes, and women too.

During the siege, Mr. Barker was kept in the hotel, expecting every moment to be killed by the furious mob. Mr. Belknap would not pay him his estimates, therefore Mr. Barker had no money with which to satisfy his men. At length the militia arrived from Burlington, and took some of the leaders prisoner, while others fled to the mountains. But a more powerful than the militia came, in the form of a Catholic priest, and they were soon all as calm as could be desired. The poor laborers were never paid, and the work was discontinued till 1849; when it began in March, and the cars commenced running in November. Seventeen Irishmen were accidentally killed while working on the road in this town.

SWIFT-WATERMEN.

Vernon   A large portion of the merchandise and productions of the eastern
Windham Co. part of the State were formerly transported in flat-bottomed
Vol. V   boats upon the Connecticut River from Hartford, Conn., to the
northern part of Vermont. Their capacity for many years was
from 10 to 20 tons, until they were increased in size to carry from
30 to 40 tons. Three men would take the boat from Hartford to
the foot of swift water, at the foot of Clary's Island, then it required 10 extra men to take the boat the next 10 miles over swift
water. These swift-water men were a hardy, energetic, jolly set
of men, ready at a moment's warning, and each received for pay
$1.50 to Brattleboro or $2.00 up to Leavitt's Rock, except during
a few years just before the cars began to do business, when the
pay was increased 50 cents to each place.

They used white ash setting poles with a heavy spike in the end,
and when there was a strong south wind they could sail a large
part of the way. At "Brattleboro tunnel" they drew the boat with
a windlass, and at Leavitt's Rock with oxen. The pay was always
the same, and when the wind was favorable, they could make two
trips a day to Brattleboro. There was also another set of men on
the New Hampshire side of the river. They usually returned in a
skiff loaded to its full capacity. Erring brothers were often tried
by a court of swift-watermen, in the usual form of sheriff, judge
and jury, and the charge to the jury was sometimes given in this
way:

"Gentlemen of the jury. You have heard the testimony of the
witnesses and the pleading of the counsel on both sides. You will
retire to your room, and after due consideration if you find the
accused guilty, say Guilty, and say no more, and, on the other
hand, if you find him *not* guilty, say Guilty and say no more."

So, the accused was brought in guilty and fined one gallon, and his accomplice, as appeared by the testimony having a hand in the offense, would be fined two gallons.

5

The Civil War Decade

Vermont gave its votes to Lincoln by a four-to-one-margin over native son Stephen A. Douglas : Baseball postponed for duration of the Civil War : State furnished 34,238 men, 91 percent of whom enlisted, to preserve the Union : Confederate raid on St. Albans from Canada in 1864 strained relations between the two countries : Vermont provided a base of operations for Fenians, Irishmen who hoped to take Canada away from the British Empire : Tourists were regarded as a mixed blessing, even in 1861 : Emigration from the state continued.

"VERMONT"

Extract from a poem delivered July 4, 1859, by E. H. Phelps:

VERMONT! ah, what music there is in the word!   *Orwell*
By us, her own children, no sweeter is heard;   *Addison Co.*
No land can be found on the face of the earth,   *Vol. 1*
So dear to our hearts as this land of our birth.
These valleys so lovely, these plenty capped hills,
And these crystaline rivers, and pure mountain rills,
And these mountains, whose summits reach upward so high
That they seem like foundations upholding the sky,
And these forest-fringed lakelets, by kind Nature given
To mirror the beauties of earth, and of heaven,

And these forests and groves, and these rugged rocks, too,
Are all dear to Vermonters, the brave and the true.
And we thank the All-Giver, Who, knowing our want,
Has favored with plenty our little Vermont.
But the sons of Vermont, ah! what can I tell
Of their valorous deeds, which ye know not full well?
They are genuine Yankees, and that is enough
To prove that they're made of the genuine stuff;
And in trade it is certain they cannot be beat.
For they make splendid bargains, and do it so neat
That you're hardly aware of the fact until told,
That in selling your goods, *you yourselves have been sold.*
And in politics, too, there is no kind of use
For me to affirm that they're "sound on the goose,"
For they all vote the ticket that seems to them best,
And with consciences pure leave to God all the rest.
They are death to oppression, and lovers of right,
For which with their lives they are willing to fight;
For look at the fields where their blood has been poured,
Where defending their homes, they have died by the sword;
Look at Bennington's field, and at Hubbardton, too,
Where they proved themselves sons of the brave and the true;
Where, cheering their comrades, they spent their last breath,
And smiled as they faced such a glorious death.
Ay, Vermont has raised heroes who'd die in the field,
Ere to foreign oppression their rights they would yield.
Such men as with Allen went over to "Ti,"
Determined to conquer, but ready to die;
Who dumfounded the foe by presenting their claim,
And took the "old fort" in Jehovah's great name.
The Vermonters are farmers, and wherever found,
You may safely conclude that they live on the ground;
For who ever knew one that didn't know how
To flourish the scythe, or to handle the plough;
And what wonderful crops are expected to grow,

When he tickles the earth with a spade or a hoe,
And what corn and potatoes, and pumpkins arise,
To cheer up his heart, and to gladden his eyes.
On all these green hill-sides, so rugged and steep,
Like a shepherd he pastures his cattle and sheep;
And, besides, he has horses as fast as the wind,
Which can leave even fleet iron horses behind.
In short, he possesses contentment of heart,
From which a king's crown would not tempt him to part.

The patriotic ardor which pervaded the North on the fall of Fort Sumter and the consequent call of the President of April 15th, 1861, for 75,000 volunteers, was as earnest and active in the town and county of Bennington in its determination to suppress the rebellion and preserve the Union, as in any part of the country. In Bennington, the flag of the stars and stripes, the symbol and representative of love of country and of the Union, was at once suspended across the street and displayed on public buildings and private dwellings. *Bennington Bennington Co. Vol. V*

The First War-Meeting

A public meeting was held on the evening of the 19th of April, filling the largest hall in town, that was attended and addressed by men of both political parties. During the meeting, news came of the massacre, on the morning of that day, of Massachusetts men on their way at the call of the President for the defence of the Capitol, by a mob of Secessionists at Baltimore. The day was re-called as the anniversary of the murdering assault on the Revolutionary patriots by the British at Lexington. The enthusiasm for sustaining the government of the Union was intense.

"The Star Spangled Banner" was sung and stirring resolutions were unanimously passed to take the most energetic measures to raise men for that purpose. Similar patriotic action was taken by other towns of the County.

Brattleboro
Windham Co.
Vol. V
In this brief presentation of incidents in the life of Mr. Frederick Holbrook may be found some of the causes of his elevation to the chair of State in 1861. During his term of office was the darkest period of our national existence. Upon no Governor of this State ever rested so grave responsibilities, or of whom was required so arduous, unremitting labors as devolved upon Governor Holbrook and his able cabinet. When gloomy croakers and defenders of rebellion were making every possible effort to weaken the already bleeding hands sustaining our old national ensign, the utterances of Vermont, through her executive, had no uncertain sound to the ear of Lincoln or to his foes.

Over 30,000 Vermont soldiers, for the Union army, confirmed those utterances and formed a living wall of steel in protection of that "Star Spangled Banner," which, in the long ago, had so often waved successful defiance to the enemies of liberty, and became a worshiped emblem of our nation's glory. The proclamations of our Governor in that period of peril, were resolute, calm and hopeful, with no sign of flinching or cessation of heavy blows at the active enemies of our government, so long as they continued such. Official declarations of this character from the northern frontier at that time, tended in no small degree to dispel the gloom oft-times surrounding the President and his cabinet. While life was in the extremities of the nation, there was reasonable hope of soundness in the body of the same. The clear light of patriotism, from the distant heights of freedom, pierced through the dark cloud of thieves, spies and assassins infesting the home of Lincoln from the beginning of the rebellion to its close.

"Gentlemen of the Senate and House of Representatives:

Grave and weighty responsibilities rest upon us in this great crisis. Let us show ourselves equal to our duties. Whatever we have to do, let us do it with one heart and one mind. However humble, we are a part of the American Union, and have a vital interest in its preservation. It is a Union consecrated to Freedom, and it falls to our lot and that of our generation to prove the ability of free-men to defend and preserve our birthright. Our institutions are passing through a baptism of blood. They must and will be maintained at whatever sacrifice; and in the momentous issue which is upon us, neither temporary reverses will discourage, nor partial successes unduly elevate us. Relying upon the incontrovertible justice of our case, the bravery, patriotism and intelligence of the soldiers of the Union, the unconquerable determination, and the spirit of American Liberty actuating the loyal people of the country, we may confidently look forward to and patiently wait the time when our beloved Republic, under the providence of God, shall be re-established in unity and power, and afford a triumphant vindication of the ability of a free people to govern themselves.

FREDERICK HOLBROOK"

George Kellogg was president of the old Savings Bank, the first chartered in the State, and one of the board of Trustees of the Vermont Asylum. For the best good of the patients, proper management and general welfare of the institution, he ever betrayed a warm and liberal interest. "The proper thing to do," was the first and uppermost question with him in every position he occupied. *Brattleboro Windham Co. Vol. V*

Though a democrat, one of the most influential and decided in the State, he disapproved of the action of the administration in the Kansas outrages, and also its action, or rather its inaction, near the commencement of the late Rebellion or Civil War. When that awful strife was fully inaugurated, he said: "I know of no other way but to stand by the old flag, come what may; all else is, with me, of secondary consideration—my party, my church may perish, but save the country."

Roxbury
Washington Co.
Vol. IV
At one time in the war, Maj. Allen Spaulding was ordered to take a small squad of men, and go in search of cattle for beef, as it had been a long time the regiment had subsisted on salt meat and "hard tack." They traveled till nearly night before they got track of what they were in quest of, and they found themselves 25 miles from camp in the enemy's territory. Being told a woman near by owned a fine flock of sheep, he took a couple of men and called on her. She with her two daughters sat on a rustic seat in a beautiful garden, surrounded with the appearances of wealth and luxury. He made known his errand, when out of her mouth poured a torrent of oaths and the coarsest invectives that he had ever heard a woman utter, abusing him and the Union army in general. A servant rode up on an elegant horse, and dismounting, asked his mistress "if she knew she was addressing Union officers?" She said she knew it very well. The Major informed her he came to buy her sheep, but as she had none to sell to "Union men," he should take them without if they suited him; and ordering one of his men to mount the horse her servant had just dismounted from, they rode off, amid the hysterical screams of the mother and daughters. They camped for the night on an old plantation, about 2 miles from there, but had pickets out to keep an eye on the movements of the enemy. After all was quiet at the plantation, 200 mounted darkies came, and attempted to retake the widow's property, but at the first crack of a rifle, they "skedaddled." The Major got back to camp with 25 head of fat cattle, and presented the beautiful pony to the Colonel.

CIVIL WAR STATISTICS FROM TWO COMMUNITIES

PLAINFIELD:
68 enlisted
5 deserted
1 killed in action
2 died of wounds
11 died of disease
12 discharged
37 served their term

STOWE:
208 men served; 40 died
12 in battle
4 wounds
1 suicide
22 disease
1 in prison

*Plainfield
Washington Co.
Vol. IV*

THE DEACON AND THE PRESIDENT

A certain Deacon in Lamoille County [Deacon Robinson, of the *Lamoille Co.* Congregational Church in Johnson—A.M.H., Ed.] having business *Vol. II* in Washington, resolved, if possible, to get a peep at President Lincoln before returning. Accordingly, he betook himself to the White House, and pressing his way through the crowd already waiting to urge their claims of one kind or another upon the good-natured President, he slipped his card into the hand of an usher, who soon announced that he had permission to enter. Upon entering the room he was accosted thus by the President, "What is *your* business, sir?" "Oh, nothing, sir," replied the Deacon, "I only called to see the President and shake hands with him." "I am glad to see you," exclaimed the President, "glad to see any one who comes on that business," at the same time giving him a hearty shake of the hand.

After exchanging a few words, the President asked him from what State he came. "From Vermont," replied the Deacon, hesitating a moment, fearing, perhaps, lest so small a place might not be known so far from home. "From Vermont!" exclaimed the President. "God bless you and your State; let me shake your hand again, sir"; whereupon he was greeted with another grip from the hand of the President, that seemed to come from the heart; after which the Deacon made way for others, and pressed out through the crowd, fully resolved that again he never would hesitate to say frankly that he came from Vermont.

BASE BALL

Pawlet
Rutland Co.
Vol. III

As if to prepare for the dread war, then impending, by a simultaneous impulse, all over the country, base ball clubs were organized during the year or two preceding 1861. Perhaps no game or exercise, outside of military drill, was ever practiced, so well calculated as this to harden the muscles and invigorate the physical functions.

Three clubs were formed in this town, in 1860–61: The Hickory, at West Pawlet, the Mettowee, at the village, and the Liberty, at North Pawlet. These several clubs engaged in the work with great spirit and earnestness and had repeated trials of skill with each other and with outside clubs. They were sustained with increasing interest until 1862, when a large portion of each club was summoned to the war when, for lack of men to play the game, they were suspended. Upon the return of peace, a new impulse has been given to the game, and the old clubs are long revived.

Stowe
Lamoille Co.
Vol. II

For some three years, the society had employed for their preacher, one-half of the time, the Rev. H. P. Cutting, then residing at Williston, Vt. For some months his labors seemed to give excellent satisfaction to the society, especially that portion who were afterwards most displeased with him. Mr. Cutting was a man of ardent temperament, and a very strong anti-slavery man. At this time the war to put down the Rebellion was becoming intense, and President Lincoln had issued his Proclamation of Emancipation. Mr. Cutting was accustomed to remember the poor slave in his public prayers, and sometimes did not refrain from a few remarks

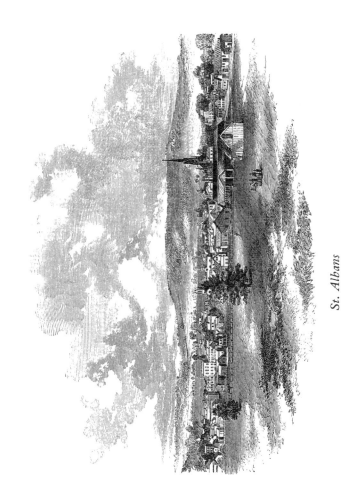

St. Albans

.

in his sermons, which those to whom they were offensive denominated "political preaching."

By special appointment at other times, he delivered one or two lectures on the affairs of the nation, as they related to the subject of Slavery, and on the Emancipation Proclamation. In these lectures, he was undoubtedly pretty severe in his denunciations of a class of persons at that time denominated Copperheads. It is altogether probable that Mr. Cutting was not always wisely discreet in what he said, and his ardency might have induced the use of language more severe than was appropriate for one accustomed to minister to persons of different political views.

The result was, that one after another of certain of his accustomed hearers vacated their pews, and some manifested their feelings by leaving church in service time. The feeling gradually grew more intense, and the disaffected ones demanded that Mr. Cutting should be dismissed, and another man employed. As a natural consequence, those whose views on the subject of slavery better accorded with Mr. Cutting's were desirous that he should not be dismissed for any such cause. By vote of the Meeting-house Association the house had been opened for use on every Sabbath. Those who favored the retention of Mr. Cutting proposed to occupy the house alternately with the other party, each sustaining the expense of its own ministrations, and the choir waiting on each. But the opponents of Mr. Cutting insisted that he should not occupy the house at all.

It so happened that a majority of the association committee were in favor of dismissing Mr. Cutting, and they accordingly waited upon him, and notified him that he could not occupy the house any more. The adherents of Mr. Cutting, who at that time claimed to have more pews in the house than his opponents, insisted that they could not be rightfully excluded from the house, especially at times when there were no other services there, and also insisted that they had a right to select their own preacher. Mr. Cutting had continued to preach in the house, statedly half the time, and occasionally his opponents had employed other preachers.

Notice was given, as usual, for Mr. Cutting to preach on a certain Sabbath. On the Saturday evening before, the choir wished to go in and practice with the organ, then but recently put in. When they came to the house they found it locked, the doors strongly barred and barricaded, and the windows fastened with screws and nails—except one, at which some persons, who had been attracted to the place, made some move to raise, and enter the house; whereupon they were met by several persons secreted in the house, who, being armed with clubs and bludgeons, beat them back in a very violent manner.

The proceeding created considerable excitement, and soon a considerable number of persons were on the ground; and being decided to go in, several seized a pole and thrust it against the door of the vestry until it fell in. The house was entered and those who had been secreted in there, soon went out. The choir commenced their exercises, and soon the house was well filled with listeners to the music, which seemed especially inspired. Measures were taken to prevent being again excluded from the house, and meeting was held there on the following Sabbath, attended by a very large congregation. Immediately after, the other party procured the sheriff, who sympathized with them, to take possession of the house, and it was again strongly barred, barricaded and bolted.

No further attempt was then made by the supporters of Mr. Cutting to occupy the house, and for some weeks they held their meetings in the old town hall—until one Sabbath, as the congregation were about to assemble for afternoon service, the doors of the new church, to the astonishment of some, came open without any noise or disturbance, and they have since held their meetings there without molestation.

This occurrence took place a few days before the session of the grand jury for the county; and an attempt was made at its session to get all who participated in any way in entering the church under the circumstances named, indicted. Bills of indictment were found against four persons on testimony which it was not deemed prudent to produce before a traverse jury, where it could be sifted, and the prosecuting officer entered a *nolle prosequi*. This schism resulted in the formation of a new society, denominated "The First Unitarian Society in Stowe," which at its organization was composed of about 100 members.

UNTIMELY DEATHS

There have been several deaths in town beside those mentioned, from suicide and accident, among whom:

Sutton Caledonia Co. Vol. 1

> Henry Allard by cutting his throat;
> Rev. Silas Wiggins by hanging;
> William O. Perham by   "
> William Carns by taking poison;
> Mrs. Silas Drown   "   "
> Betsey Ball by   "   "
> Reuben Ash by a tree falling on him;
> Moses Morrill, a   "   "   "   "

The first general business of the county and article of commerce was potash, or salts of lye, which was made in every town. The second business, as grain became abundant, was the distillation of liquors. Distilleries were erected and the whisky trade carried on very extensively. At one time there were 10 distilleries in operation in Cambridge. Their liquors were trafficked off at Montreal. Then raising hemp succeeded, for dressing of which for market, a large factory was erected at Waterville, but the business soon became worthless, leaving a large amount on the farmers' hands, and the factory was turned into a woolen mill. There have been 5 factories in the county, but fire has destroyed two of the largest at Waterville, which are now being rebuilt (1869).

Lamoille Co. Vol. II

The manufacture of starch from potatoes came up next. There have been 19 factories in the county which have made large quantities of starch. In the west part of the county the business has partly stopped now; two factories have been burned, and four have ceased to run. The hop culture has also been quite extensively carried on, but the price being now low, many have destroyed their hop yards, and butter and cheese making has come in to take the place, probably to much more permanent advantage. Maple sugar is also greatly improved in quality and every year the sugar orchards are bettered, the old fashion kettle and sap-trough have disappeared and a good arch and neat sap-pans with a house to enclose them succeeded.

Linseed oil was also made in Morristown at one time, but for some unknown reason did not operate well; and in a short time the business was abandoned.

Fairfax In 1811, the number of school districts maintaining schools was
Franklin Co. 11, and the number of scholars returned was 466, showing a
Vol. II rapid increase in the early settlement of the town.

In the year 1861 the number of school districts making returns and sustaining schools was 17, and the number of scholars of all ages attending school was 475, showing but small increase in scholars for the half-century following 1811. This must be accounted for partly in the difference of the school laws, the old law requiring all children between the ages of 4 and 18 to be returned, whilst the present law only requires those who attend school. Another reason is, that many of the young men emigrate early to the tempting West, and there settle. The first frame school-house built, was in the village near the stone dwelling of the late Gen. Grout.

One hundred and twenty years ago, or in 1771—three years *Newfane*
before its organization as a town—there were 52 inhabitants in *Windham Co.*
Newfane. By the several U.S. censuses the population of the town *Vol. V*
is given as follows: 1791—660; 1800—1,000; 1810—1,276; 1820—
1,506; 1830—1,441; 1840—1,403; 1850—1,304; 1860—1,191; 1870
—1,113; 1880—1,031; 1890—952.

These figures show a loss of population in each decade since
1820, and a total loss of 554 since that date. The decline of population in Newfane has something more than a local interest, for
similar conditions have led to a like result in more than half the
towns of the State. A loss of population occurred generally in
the farming towns; only two towns in Windham County (Brattleboro and Rockingham) have as large a population as they
had sixty years ago, and the growth of these two is in their pros-
perous villages. The loss of population in Newfane cannot justly
be accredited to the want of a fertile soil or less attractive homes
than can generally be found elsewhere. Statistics of agricultural
products and their values prove beyond refutation that the
farmers of Vermont realize more profit from their labor and in-
vestments than the average farmer in any one of more than thirty
other States, yet our people emigrate and often settle in a less
desirable country than they leave.

There are two direct causes for the decrease of population in
Newfane, which, without seeking for any precedent cause, fully
account for it; these are: (1) a low birth rate; (2) emigration.
In the early history of the town families of from eight to twelve
children were not uncommon. At this time it is rare to find a
family with more than four or five children, and a large number
of families have none. The average number of persons in a Newfane family, as found by the census of 1890, was only 3.76. The
average annual birth rate in the United States is estimated by
good authorities at about 35 per thousand of living inhabitants.
The average number of births in Newfane for the past 30 years,
as shown by a compilation from the registration reports, was as
follows:

Average annual number of births for ten years ending with 1870—17.7; 1880—17.1; 1890—17.

Average annual births for 30 years, 17.27.

At the normal birth rate the whole number of births in 30 years would have been about 1,155.

The whole number of births in the past 30 years was 518.

The deficiency is 637.

There are no complete records from which the birth rate at the time when the town had more than 1,500 inhabitants can be ascertained, but it was then, probably, above rather than below the normal rate, or more than twice as great as at the present time. In 1824 the number of children in the common schools of Newfane, as stated in the town history, was 518. Last year (1890) the number of scholars in town attending any school was 184. In 1824 the children in the schools were 34.5 per cent of the total population; they are now but 19.3 per cent.

CRIME.

Lamoille Co. *Vol. II* There has been as yet no convictment for capital crimes in this County. In 1867, two men in Eden—McDowell and Finnegan—got to differing about some land, when a quarrel arose and they went at each other with axes. The fight was short and McDowell received a slight wound when he buried his axe in Finnegan's side, which caused death in one hour. At the County court McDowell was set at liberty upon the ground that it was in self-defence, and if he had not struck a fatal blow, Finnegan would.

Lamoille Co. *Vol. II* There reside in Elmore a Mr. and Mrs Barnes, who live alone, and carry on their farm, with the exception of a few days work in the spring and haying. Mr. Barnes is 87 years of age and has a stock consisting of ten head of cattle, ten sheep, and one horse; he has

The Green at Woodstock

fed his stock and milked six cows, the coldest weather we have had this winter (186–) without going to the house.

Mrs. Barnes is 81 years of age, does all the necessary work of a farmer's wife, and thinks nothing of walking three or four miles and back. When she was 77 she walked on a snow-path 26 miles in one day. At 79 she came from Montpelier after 3 o'clock, P.M., and arrived at her son's in Elmore, a distance of 15 miles, at 12 o'clock at night—she walking it.

ELIPHALET JOHNSON.

Born in Chesterfield, N.H., about 1781, he spent the last 50 years of his life mostly in the east village of Brattleboro. His parentage was respectable, but he was partially blind and so unfortunate in his general organization, he had not the ability to properly take care of himself. The labor he engaged in was generally for those the least able to reward him. He found lodgings in some barn or out-house, and during his last years depended mainly upon charity. If any boy insulted him, as they frequently did, Johnson always felt certain the father of that boy would in some way come to grief, by failure in business or some family affliction. *Brattleboro Windham Co. Vol. V*

Not withstanding his menial occupation, lack of culture, and unprepossessing externals, he often attracted attention by his quaint remarks and ingenious poetical compositions. Returning disgusted from Nauvoo, wither he was enticed by a Mormon brother, he encountered a fearful storm on Lake Erie, and wrote:

> As o'er Lake Erie's boisterous wave,
>   I fearfully was driven,
> I thought each billow was my grave,
>   And pray'd to be forgiven.
>
> Then did I promise to my God,
>   If safe again on shore,
> I'd be submissive to his rod,
>   And leave the land no more.

Johnson was not a sot, but like many sons of genius that have preceded him, had a fondness for liquid sources of inspiration and yellow snuff, that may have been indispensable to his peculiar mental exercises.

But his happiest efforts were reserved for New Year's or Fourth of July. He was ever seeking for some sin with which to charge the Democratic party. From the days of Jackson, in 1829, to President Polk's administration, in 1847, we frequently heard his denunciations. Soon after Van Buren became President, Johnson gave him the following compliment:

> Martin Van Buren—designing man,
>   With Andrew Jackson laid the plan
> To make retrenchment but a sham,
>   And strain our country black as Ham.

In 1847 we were fighting Mexico. News came of the bombardment of Vera Cruz. Invited on July 4th to give his toast, his bent, aged frame shook with emotion, tears flowed down his withered face, and from quivering lips came feebly forth his first four lines. Warming with the theme, firmer and firmer rose his voice as he proceeded, and when he recited the last line his upraised right foot came down with a vengeance to the floor:

> This glorious day has come again,
>   The proudest day for freedom's son,
> For then a tyrant's galling chain
>   Broke on the soil our father's won.

> But now the cries of Mexan daughters,
>   With mangled limbs at Vera Cruz;
> They tell how freemen's hands can slaughter,
>   How independence they abuse.

> Go, Democrat! bow low your head,
>   Heaven may forgive you this disgrace,
> But history's page you've made so red,
>   All hell and Polk cannot efface.

Coming now to speak of what man has done for Burlington, it *Burlington*
becomes us to be more modest. The city is built upon eight streets *Chittenden Co.*
running parallel to the Lake, crossed by four running up from the *Vol. 1*
lake to the College Hill, and by several shorter ones. It can hardly
be claimed for Burlington that it has any architecture. Its public
buildings are creditable, many of them; but none are conspicuous
for their architectural beauty, if we except two or three of the
churches. In private dwellings, Burlington displays considerable
taste and luxury. The style which prevails in the more ambitious
residences approaches as nearly to the Italian Villa as anything—
that is, a square house with three unencumbered fronts, and with a
belvedere on the roof: a mode of building which seems to have
been prompted by the desire to make the most of the fine pros-
pects in so many different directions. A stranger coming from
almost any other New England village of corresponding size and
wealth, would probably be struck with the absence of the con-
fectioner's Gothic, now so prevalent.

Burlington is not yet old enough to have a very luxuriant dis-
play of shade trees along its streets and in its parks. If we had
been spared the ravages of the borer, the locust trees of Burlington would have rivaled the elms of New Haven and the maples of
Stockbridge. Twenty years ago but few trees of other kinds were
to be seen in our streets, but by degrees they have almost all given
place to elms, basswoods and horse chestnuts, and but for the
temporary nudity of our side-walks, there would be no reason to
regret the change.

Thirty-five years ago, one would not have been thought extravagant if he had predicted such a growth of commercial prosperity as should in time make Burlington one of the business
capitals of the North. Having direct and easy water communication with New York on the one hand, and with the under-
developed region through which flow the waters of the Great
Lakes on the other; being the natural point of communication

between a large inland tract, rich in agricultural products, and
the highway by which those products could be transmitted to the
markets, and the commodities for which they are exchanged
could be returned for distribution, Burlington seemed intended
by Nature to be the great commercial *entrepôt* for this section of
territory. With such expectations, capital was gradually coming
in, and a considerable wholesale trade was being built up, when
the opening of the railroads changed the whole current of things,
and for a time seemed likely to rob Burlington entirely of any
commercial importance.

Direct communication was opened between the southern cities
and every town on the railroad; there was no further need of a
central forwarding station between the rural producer or country
store-keeper and the market; traffic rushed by us to its ultimate
destination each way, and Burlington was a mere way-station.
Thus died out one kind of business on which the future commercial growth of Burlington was supposed to depend, and for
many years she did not recover, and some thought she never
would recover her old relative position, far less make any considerable progress. One advantage, however, was left to her, and
we are only just beginning to see how valuable an advantage it
is, viz: Burlington is the only point on the Lake from the extreme southern to the extreme northern limits of the State, at
which the railroad and lake navigation come together. The importance of this fact, connected with the territorial advantages
above alluded to, will at once be seen on reflection; although, as
was hinted above, its value was not practically appreciated for
many years after the railroads were opened, and is even now but
partially turned to account.

This is the simple and natural explanation of the almost wonderful revival of enterprise here within five years past; this accounts
for such a vast accumulation of lumber that not only our wharves
will not hold it, but the bay will hardly furnish room enough to
build all the wharves that are needed; this justifies the transfer of
large iron works from an inland region traversed only by common

roads, to a point where the bulky raw material can be brought by water and from which the manufactured article can be hurried to market by rail. And this, unless we are greatly mistaken, will yet, ere very many years, actually make Burlington what she bade fair to be thirty-five years ago, and what she despaired of ever being fifteen years ago: one of the most important business centers in northern New England.

Burlington has not yet become to any considerable extent (may it never be) a country residence for wealthy families from the cities.* Perhaps it is so remote as to be out of danger. Let us hope that it is. Let us do all we can to keep up the notion among our city cousins, that to live "away up in Vermont," is the American equivalent for being exiled to Siberia. Let us tell them that we like to have them *visit* us during the few fleeting days in mid-summer when we can safely walk about with them in our fields without our buffalo coats and bear-skin gowns, but that *they* belong to altogether too delicate a race to think of *living through* our severe summers with any comfort.

Not that we do not think very highly of our city cousins, especially *when we see them in the city*. But when they come with their long baggage-train of trunks and band-boxes, and take possession of a country village, bringing their livery and their minister with them, occupying all the finest building sites, ordering all their groceries and toggery from the city, and importing into industrious communities the seductive fashion of doing nothing and doing it elegantly, they turn the heads of the young, demoralize the whole tone of society, convert respectable villages into the likeness of suburban Connecticut and New Jersey, and for all these losses do not compensate by adding any appreciable amount to the circulating capital or to public improvement.

* The writer certainly does not intend to reflect upon the two or three families from the city already residing among us, whose enterprise and taste have done so much to beautify our city. He had in mind what he has witnessed in certain villages in the southern part of the State.

Chronology

of VERMONT *to* 1872

by ESTHER MUNROE SWIFT

1609 Champlain explored the lake which is named for him and fought Iroquois on western bank.

1666 French built Fort St. Anne on Isle La Motte.

1690 First English settlements at Chimney Point and at Vernon (then part of Northfield, Mass.).

1704 Indians raided Deerfield, Mass. Captive Rev. John Williams preached a sermon to fellow prisoners on Williams River near Rockingham in Vermont en route north.

1715 Equivalent Lands granted by Massachusetts to Connecticut in payment for Connecticut land Massachusetts had mistakenly settled.

1724 Massachusetts built first permanent settlement in present Vermont, at Fort Dummer, in southeastern corner of the state.

1726 Timothy Dwight (father of later Yale president with same name) first white child known to have been born in Vermont (Fort Dummer).

1741 Boundary between Massachusetts and New Hampshire surveyed (later became border between Massachusetts and Vermont).

1745 Massachusetts built outpost fort on "Great Meadow" in Putney.

1749 Bennington first town granted in present-day Vermont by Governor Benning Wentworth of New Hampshire.

1745 Beginning of second French and Indian War. Baby "Captive" Johnson born in wilderness of Cavendish following mother's capture at Fort Number 4 (Charlestown, N.H.).

1759 Rogers' Rangers raided village of St. Francis Indians in Canada. British took Lake Champlain forts at Ticonderoga and Crown Point from French. Crown Point Road, from Connecticut River to Lake Champlain, begun.

1760–63 Governor Wentworth of New Hampshire made 138 grants in Vermont, hence area became known as the Hampshire Grants.

1761 Formal settlement of Bennington begun.

1762 First Congregational church in Vermont established in Bennington.

1763 Treaty of Paris marked end of French and Indian War. France relinquished claims to Vermont.

1764 King George III proclaimed Connecticut River "to be" boundary between New York and New Hampshire. New York called Wentworth's earlier grants null and void and expected settlers to re-buy their land from the New York colony.

1765 Settlers convened in Bennington, concerned over the status of their New Hampshire grants.

1768 First Baptist church in Vermont organized at Shaftsbury. Cumberland County (partly in Vermont) created by New York in effort to establish jurisdiction over the Hampshire Grants settlers.

1769 New York surveyors sent back home from Bennington by settlers.

1770 Green Mountain Boys organized to combat New York land claims.

1771 Sheriff Ten Eyck of Albany, N.Y., failed to eject a Grants landholder from the settler's Bennington farm.

1773 Fort Frederick built at Winooski Falls by Ira Allen and his cousin, Remember Baker.

1774 New York Governor Tryon offered £50 reward each for the capture of Green Mountain Boys leaders.

1775 "Massacre" of William French and Daniel Houghton, when Yorkers tried to take Westminster Courthouse in order to bring criminal proceedings against Green Mountain Boys.

Old Catamount Tavern, Bennington.

Battle of Lexington and Concord (Mass.). Ethan Allen captured Fort Ticonderoga and Seth Warner took Crown Point. Continental Congress convened and Committee of Safety formed.

1776   American Declaration of Independence. British-American naval battles on Lake Champlain. Hubbardton Military Road built.

1777   Battles of Hubbardton and Bennington. Indian raid on Brandon. Name "Vermont" first suggested to state's founding fathers by Dr. Thomas Young of Philadelphia. Vermont's Declaration of Independence and Constitution adopted.

1777–91   Vermont, as an independent republic, established its own coinage, weights and measures, postal service and militia.

1778 First general elections in Vermont. Thomas Chittenden elected
      first Governor of Vermont. First legislature met in Windsor.
      Bennington and Windham counties established.

1779 Vermont state seal designed (it is thought) by Ira Allen. Bayley-
      Hazen Road, from Newbury to Westfield, completed.

1780 Royalton burned by Indians, incited by British.

1781 Rutland, Windsor and Orange counties established. *The Ver-
      mont Gazette, or Green Mountain Post Boy*, first Vermont
      newspaper, published at Westminster on Stephen Daye press
      (discontinued in 1783). "Haldimand negotiations" between
      Vermont leaders and British in Canada, concerning Ver-
      mont's status as an independent entity. Cornwallis surrendered
      at Yorktown and the Revolutionary War was over.

1782–83 New Hampshire and New York continued to bicker over
      Vermont. Vermont petitioned Congress for admission to
      the Union.

1783 "Guilford War," instigated by York-minded townspeople, put
      down by Ethan Allen and Vermont militia.

1784 Ethan Allen published *Reason, the Only Oracle of Man . . .* ,
      an attack on organized Christianity.

1785 Addison became the state's first incorporated county. First
      marble quarry in United States opened in Dorset. Reuben
      Harmon, at Rupert, began minting coins stamped *Republic
      of Vermont.*

1787 Chittenden County, named for first governor, established.

1789 George Washington became first President of the United
      States. Ethan Allen died in Burlington. State's first wagon
      road—from Vergennes City to Montpelier—finished.

1790 Vermont and New York agreed on $30,000 indemnity to be
      paid to N.Y. residents for land they had lost in Vermont.
      Prince Edward, later Duke of Kent and father of Queen
      Victoria, traveled through Vermont en route to Boston from
      Canada. United States Patent Number 1 issued to Samuel
      Hopkins of Burlington for a method of making potash.

1791 Vermont admitted to the Union as 14th state. Second United
      States Congress in session. Political parties were Federalists
      and Democratic Republicans (the latter were first called
      Republicans, but later just Democrats). Vermont's population

was 85,539 in 185 towns—of which Guilford was the largest, with 2,432 people. First library in Vermont established at Brookfield. First Presbyterian church in Vermont built at Ryegate. Justin Morgan, the school teacher, brought his horse (renamed Justin Morgan, and to become the foundation sire of the Morgan breed) to Vermont.

1792 Franklin, Caledonia, Essex and Orleans counties incorporated.

1793 Samuel Morey of Fairlee operated his steamboat on the Connecticut River—14 years before Fulton's *Clermont* on the Hudson River. First Methodist church in Vermont established at Danby. First copper mine in the United States opened in Strafford. First pottery made in Vermont at Bennington factory.

1794 First Universalist church in Vermont organized at Barnard. *Rutland Herald*, the state's oldest newspaper in continuous publication, was begun.

1796 John Adams, Federalist, elected President. First turnpike company organized in Vermont to build road from Bennington to Wilmington.

1797 Thomas Chittenden, Vermont's first Governor, died.

1798 Matthew Lyon was re-elected to Congress while serving a jail term at Vergennes. Lorenzo Dow, the celebrated itinerant Methodist minister, preached in the Essex County circuit, north and west of Burlington.

1800 Thomas Jefferson, Democratic Republican, was elected President, and began the practice of displacing political opponents from federal office (Vermont had voted for Adams). Vermont's population was 154,465 in 226 towns, with Guilford still the largest. Middlebury College and University of Vermont were opened.

1801 Brigham Young, Mormon leader, born in Whitingham.

1802 Grand Isle County established. First canal in the United States built at Bellows Falls. Thomas Davenport, inventor of the electric motor, born in Williamstown.

1803 State flag adopted. Judge Theophilus Harrington of Clarendon ruled that the only proof of ownership of a slave was a "bill of sale from Almighty God."

1804 Jefferson re-elected President.

1805 Joseph Smith, Mormon founder, born in Sharon.
1806 State banks established at Middlebury and Woodstock (closed in 1811).
1807 State penitentiary established at Windsor.
1808 James Madison, Democratic Republican, elected President. First Lake Champlain steamboat in operation one year after Fulton's *Clermont*. Montpelier became state capital and first State House (wooden) built. Temperance movement in United States began with founding of National Temperance Society at Saratoga, N.Y.
1810 Vermont's population was 217,895, with Windsor the largest town. Washington County incorporated as *Jefferson* (name changed in 1814).
1811 William Jarvis of Weathersfield, U.S. Consul to Portugal, introduced Merino sheep to this country.
1812 Madison re-elected President. Beginning of war (not popular in Vermont) with Great Britain. First Sunday school in Vermont held in Concord.
1813 Governor Martin Chittenden withdrew Vermont militia from deployment at Plattsburgh, N.Y., as a gesture of dissatisfaction with the war. Stephen A. Douglas, the political leader known as the "Little Giant," born at Brandon. First glass factory in Vermont begun at Salisbury. Vermont Medical Society incorporated.
1814 Macdonough defeated British naval forces at Plattsburgh, N.Y. Ira Allen died a pauper in Philadelphia.
1815 End of War of 1812.
1816 The year without a summer, known as "Eighteen-hundred-and-froze-to-death." James Monroe, Republican, elected President, beginning the "era of good feeling."
1817 President Monroe visited Vermont. First carpenter's squares made in United States were manufactured in Shaftsbury by their inventor, Silas Hawes.
1818 First medical school in Vermont begun at Castleton.
1819 Norwich University established at Norwich (later moved to Northfield).
1820 Monroe re-elected President. Vermont's population 235,966;

Windsor still the largest town. Vermont protested admission to the Union of Missouri as a slave state.

1821 First medical school at state university opened.

1823 Canal from Lake Champlain to Hudson River opened to traffic. First teachers' training school in United States begun in Concord.

1824 John Quincy Adams, National Republican, elected President.

1825 Lafayette toured Vermont and effected release of Revolutionary war hero General Barton, who had served 14 years in jail for debt. Erie Canal opened and Vermonters began emigrating to newly opened western lands.

1826 American Temperance Society founded at Boston (*see also* 1808). First Lake Champlain lighthouse built on Juniper Island.

1827 Vermont Mutual Fire Insurance Company of Montpelier (nation's oldest such organization in continuous operation) founded.

1828 Democratic Republicans became Democrats; Federalists had disappeared; Whigs, National Republicans and Anti-Masons had appeared. Andrew Jackson, Democrat, elected President (Vermont votes went to John Quincy Adams, as the National Republican candidate.) William Lloyd Garrison in Bennington edited *Journal of the Times*, advocating anti-slavery, temperance, peace and moral reform.

1829 Beginning of Anti-Mason era in Vermont.

1830 Vermont's population 280,652, with Middlebury the largest town. Thaddeus Fairbanks of St. Johnsbury invented the platform scale. Beginning of sheep-raising boom in Vermont, lasting until after the Civil War. Chester A. Arthur, twenty-first President of the United States, born at Fairfield.

1831 William A. Palmer elected Governor of Vermont on the Anti-Masonic platform and re-elected each year through 1834.

1832 Jackson re-elected President (Vermont's Presidential votes went to William Wirt, the Anti-Masonic party candidate).

1833 Second State House (brick and granite) built at Montpelier. First Roman Catholic church in Vermont established at Burlington.

1834 Vermont Anti-Slavery Society formed.

1835 Lamoille County incorporated.

1836 Martin Van Buren, Democrat, elected President of the United States. Vermont created Senate to replace Governor's Council. Marble first quarried in West Rutland. Brattleboro Retreat established as an insane asylum.

1836–37 National money panic and wheat failures resulted in suspension of specie payments and riots by "bread mobs" throughout the country.

1837 Vermont protested slave trade in District of Columbia. Insurgents of the Patriot Movement for conquest of Canada surrendered to U.S. Army in Vermont.

1838 Congress passed Gag Law to deny hearing anti-slavery protests from Vermont and other abolitionist states. John Humphrey Noyes, later founder of New York Oneida Community, established at Putney a community based on "Bible Communism" or "complex marriage" (Vermonters called it wife-swapping).

1839 The national Liberty, or Anti-Slavery, Party made its first Presidential nomination. Slate first quarried in Vermont at Fair Haven.

1840 Vermont's population 291,948, with Burlington the largest town. William H. Harrison, Democrat, elected President (Vermont's votes went to Daniel Webster). Vermont legislature enacted law allowing escaped slaves a trial by jury.

1841 Anti-Slavery Party made its first nomination for Vermont Governor.

1841–42 More anti-slavery protests to Congress from Vermont, and state asked for U.S. Constitutional amendment that would abolish slavery.

1842 "Vermont epidemic"—a disease similar to erysipelas—caused thousands of deaths, with many burials not until the following spring.

1843 Vermont legislature passed law making it illegal to recover escaped slaves in Vermont. Vermont legislature voted money for establishment of agricultural societies.

1843–44 Millerites, an emotional religious sect, decided the world was going to end and gave away all their property.

1844   James K. Polk, Democrat, elected President. Vermont passed its first liquor-control law, fixing fees for licenses and appointing county commissioners to issue them.

1846   United States at war with Mexico (not popular in Vermont because it would add more slave territory). Estey organs first made at Brattleboro. Vermont liquor-control law extended to allow vote at town level on licenses (still in effect).

1848   Zachary Taylor, Whig, elected President. Free Soil Party was organized and Liberty Party merged with it. Martin Van Buren was the Liberty candidate for the Presidency.

1848–49   First railroads in state opened to traffic from Rutland to Burlington, and White River Junction to Bethel.

1849   Vermont legislature declared slavery to be a "crime against humanity."

1850   Vermont's population 314,120; Burlington the largest town. Additional liquor-control laws passed by Vermont. Vermont state's attorneys instructed by law to defend escaped slaves in Vermont who were claimed by their masters.

1852   Franklin Pierce, Democrat, elected President (opposed by Winfield Scott as a Whig, and John P. Hale as a Free Soiler). Vermont's first full prohibition law prohibited the sale of intoxicants of any kind except for "medicinal, chemical or mechanical" uses. Opponents of slavery became known as Republicans.

1856   James Buchanan elected President (John Frémont, "The Pathfinder," the Republican candidate, received three-fourths of Vermont's votes). Vermont legislature appropriated $20,000 for the relief of anti-slave men in Kansas, then rescinded the act the following year.

1857   Vermont legislative resolution condemned the Dred Scott decision of the U.S. Supreme Court. Second State House at Montpelier burned.

1858   Vermont wrote her own emancipation proclamation, saying that all Negroes in the state, or thereafter brought in, would be free.

1859   Third (and present) State House built at Montpelier. John Dewey, philosopher and educator, born at Burlington. Abby Maria Hemenway's historical magazine entered according to

Act of Congress in the Clerk's Office of the District Court, District of Vermont.

1860 Vermont's population 315,098; Burlington the largest town. Abraham Lincoln elected President, receiving most Vermont votes even though Stephen A. Douglas, his opponent, was Vermont-born and had campaigned in the state. Secession ordinances passed by Southern states. Vermont militia prepared for war.

1861–64 The Civil War was to Vermont almost an holy war: half the state's eligible men served, and 25 percent died as a result, leaving the state short of adult men in the postwar years.

1862 U.S. Congress passed Vermont Senator Morrill's land-grant college act. William Scott, the young Vermonter known as "The Sleeping Sentry," who was pardoned by Lincoln, died at the Battle of Lee's Mills.

1864 Raid on St. Albans by Confederate guerillas seeking to bolster Southern finances and morale.

1866–70 Fenian Raids on Canada from Vermont bases by Irish who sought to take Canada from Britain.

1867 Morrill Tariff Act protected United States wool market and agriculture.

1868 Ulysses S. Grant, Republican, elected President (Vermont vote was overwhelmingly Republican).

1870 Vermont's population 330,551; Burlington, by then an incorporated city, still the largest community in the state. Vermont Constitutional Convention proposed amendments to state constitution, doing away with Council of Censors (which had had the right to veto legislative actions) and making both legislative sessions and state elections biennial.

1871 Proposed amendments ratified by people of Vermont.

1872 Calvin Coolidge, thirtieth President of the United States, born at Plymouth, Vermont.

Index

The Index entries below are limited to the material excerpted from Abby Hemenway's *Gazetteer* itself, and the place names cited are Vermont town names unless otherwise indicated. To further orient the reader, we call attention to the notes preceding each chapter and to the Chronology beginning on page 165.